Royal Tours
1786–2010

ARTHUR BOUSFIELD AND GARRY TOFFOLI

Home to Canada

Royal Tours

1786–2010

DUNDURN PRESS

TORONTO

Editor: Cheryl Hawley
Design: Jennifer Scott
Printer: Friesens

Library and Archives Canada Cataloguing in Publication

Bousfield, Arthur, 1943-
     Royal tours, 1786-2010 : home to Canada / by Arthur Bousfield and Garry Toffoli.

Issued also in an electronic format.
ISBN 978-1-55488-800-9

1. Visits of state--Canada. 2. Royal visitors--Canada. I. Toffoli, Garry, 1953- II. Title.

FC223.R6B69 2010   394'.40971   C2010-902410-9

1   2   3   4   5   14   13   12   11   10

We acknowledge the support of the **Canada Council for the Arts** and the **Ontario
Arts Council** for our publishing program. We also acknowledge the financial support
of the **Government of Canada** through the **Canada Book Fund** and **The Association
for the Export of Canadian Books**, and the **Government of Ontario** through the
Ontario Book Publishers Tax Credit program, and the **Ontario Media Development
Corporation**.

Printed and bound in Canada.
www.dundurn.com

Dundurn Press
3 Church Street, Suite 500
Toronto, Ontario, Canada
M5E 1M2

Gazelle Book Services Limited
White Cross Mills
High Town, Lancaster, England
LA1 4XS

Dundurn Press
2250 Military Road
Tonawanda, NY
U.S.A. 14150

To

RICHARD MICHAEL TOPOROSKI

Ukrainian Catholic, Doctor of Philosophy, retired Associate Professor of Classics,
royalist, constitutionalist, writer, public speaker, British Columbian
who over many years and in a diversity of ways
has been a mentor and friend of the authors

CONTENTS

ACKNOWLEDGEMENTS

THE AUTHORS ARE INDEBTED to the chairman and board of the Canadian Royal Heritage Trust/ Fondation du patrimoine royal du Canada for allowing them to use many pictures from the King Louis XIV Canadian Royal Heritage Archives and the King George III Canadian Royal Heritage Library. There are also many individuals who have helped with the book to whom the authors owe and wish to express their gratitude. Janet Huse generously and graciously took pictures of the Toronto portion of Her Majesty the Queen's 2010 tour, as she has in the past of royal tours for other works by the authors. Lynne Bell put photos of many Canadian royal tours she has covered as a journalist at their service. Other pictures by *Monarchy Canada* photographers were also used. Dr. Christopher McCreery, M.V.O., secretary to the lieutenant-governor of Nova Scotia, and Mr. Michael Laffin, manager of Province House, facilitated obtaining several important historic Nova Scotia royal pictures as illustrations. Garry Shutlak, senior archivist Public Services, Nova Scotia Archives, arranged the use of the miniature of Madame de St. Laurent. Mrs. Barbara Rusch, the "ephemera diva," permitted the authors to reproduce two pages from the Duke of Kent's letter in her collection and surprised them with the droll trade advertisement bearing the colour images of the Duke and Duchess of Kent. All uncredited illustrations in this book are from the public domain. The kindness — serendipitous in origin — of Mr. Robert McWilliams in allowing access to the notes of his great-granduncle, Honourable Roland McWilliams, lieutenant-governor of Manitoba, and great-grandaunt, Mrs. (Margaret) McWilliams, and use of pictures of the Earl of Athlone, HRH Princess Alice, HRH the Duke of Kent, and HRH the Princess Elizabeth (Queen Elizabeth II) in the McWilliams Papers is gratefully acknowledged. Rachelle Ross, archivist of the Great-West Life Assurance Company, was especially helpful in locating the Canada Life painting by A.J. Casson and granting leave for its inclusion. The Currency Museum of the Bank of Canada kindly supplied the picture of the 1917 dollar in the National Currency Collection bearing the image of HRH Princess Patricia of Connaught (Lady Patricia Ramsay). Jim Allan and Bob Gilbert facilitated photographing of the Orillia Hunt mural at Parkwood depicting the Prince of Wales and Colonel R.S. "Sam" McLaughlin.

INTRODUCTION

WHEN QUEEN ELIZABETH II left California for British Columbia in 1983, she said that she was "going home to Canada." She was not the first member of the royal family to call Canada her home. This book relates the Canadian stories of eleven senior members of the royal family who were or would become monarch, viceroy, chatelaine, or commander-in-chief, together with their eight consorts and members of their immediate families who came to Canada. They all called and made Canada "home."

Since Canada's pioneer days, members of the royal family have been making the country their home through residence, public service, and naval and military duty. Sometimes only for the space of a journey, sometimes for several years, princes, princesses, near or remote heirs to the throne, future monarchs or actual sovereigns, the royalties identified themselves intimately with the folk and life of the land. Four centuries of Canada's history — the eighteenth to the twenty-first — are bridged by their journeys. Space limits the members of Canada's royal family whose stories can be described in this account, so it must be noted here that dozens of other royalties have, in the past and the present, made homes in Canada for various lengths of time and purposes. This book is a representative, not a comprehensive, account of the royal family in Canada.

In order to tour, many royal travellers crossed the ocean; others began their journeys from short-term Canadian homes. They made their way through the length and breadth of a land of constantly stretching borders. Their routes were covered by means as varied as the transportation technology of the day allowed: jet, calèche, batteau, helicopter, curricle, car, horseback, prairie wagon, train, sleigh, tram, warship, loggers' raft, royal yacht, steamship, and ocean liner.

Besides influencing Canada's development in important ways, royal tours often changed the royalties' lives. Official tour, private holiday, exercise of the office of governor general, or military service, whatever they undertook was exacting. They could find themselves quelling a riot, meting out justice, opening a bridge, or perhaps shaping a nationality, ameliorating foreign relations, bringing a ray of hope to minorities, lifting public life for a few precious moments above the mundane or divisive political fray. Some royalties arguably executed their duties better than others; none showed neglect or disdain for the people among whom they moved.

Abroad, their tours showcased Canada. To Canadians at home, by causing communities large and small to put their best foot forward, they revealed the immensity, diversity, and grandeur of the country. Royal journeys provide glimpses of Canadian life and people that otherwise would never be recorded. Royal tours are as Canadian as a hockey game — and even older.

Today the growing perception that Canadians have become disconnected from their history is troubling With the bicentenary of the War of 1812 — Canada's "War of Independence" — and the Diamond Jubilee of the queen's reign drawing nearer, *Royal Tours 1786– 2010: Home to Canada* attempts to help remedy that.

THE QUEEN IN CANADA

June 28 to July 6, 2010

The royal couple at the "Celebration of Nova Scotia," Halifax, June 29. Both the queen and Duke of Edinburgh enjoy their official life. A team approach is the technique they have successfully applied to reigning.

The queen waved to acknowledge the salutes from sailors as she inspected the international fleet review in Halifax, marking the one hundredth anniversary of the Royal Canadian Navy.

At a ceremony in Rideau Hall on June 30, the queen unveiled the model of a new image of herself that will be carved on a pillar in the Senate foyer, to join those of previous sovereigns of Canada.

Tim Rooke/Rex Features

"I wish you all the very happiest Canada Day. God bless you all and God bless Canada," was the message when Elizabeth II, Queen of Canada, spoke to the nation from the 2010 Canada Day ceremonies on Parliament Hill, Ottawa.

Janet Huse, Monarchy Canada Photo

The queen greeted Hazel McCallion, the colourful eighty-nine-year-old mayor of Mississauga, Canada's sixth largest city, on disembarking at Pearson International Airport for the Toronto portion of her tour, July 3.

Janet Huse, Monarchy Canada Photo

At her official arrival in Ontario the queen spoke to her representative in the province, Honourable David Onley.

Escorted by the Dean, Very Reverend Douglas Stoute, the queen and Duke of Edinburgh arrived at St. James' Anglican Cathedral on Sunday morning, July 4.

Janet Huse, Monarchy Canada Photo

Leaving St. James' Cathedral, Her Majesty accepted a gift from a representative of the Native people. At the cathedral the queen gave sets of eight silver hand bells to the two chapels royal of the Mohawks in Canada, to mark the three hundredth anniversary of Queen Anne's reception of the Four Indian Kings at court.

Janet Huse, Monarchy Canada Photo

Escorted by the Toronto Police Mounted Unit, and RCMP postilions, the queen and Duke of Edinburgh arrived by landau in bright sunlight and extreme heat at Woodbine Race Track for the running of the Queen's Plate.

Janet Huse, Monarchy Canada Photo

Janet Huse, Monarchy Canada Photo

Left: *The queen, flanked by purple and silver hangings with her royal cypher E II R and royal coat of arms for Canada, made a nationwide address at the state dinner in Toronto.*

Below: *At the state dinner the queen unveiled a new Hockey Hall of Fame exhibit with her own Team Canada jersey.*

Janet Huse, Monarchy Canada Photo

Facing Page: *The queen inspected a composite guard of honour at Queen's Park on July 6, comprised of soldiers from several regiments in Southern Ontario, of which Her Majesty and the Duke of Edinburgh are colonels-in-chief.*

At Queen's Park in Toronto on July 6, the queen unveiled a plaque for the 150th anniversary of the naming of the park after her great-great-grandmother, Queen Victoria, by her great-grandfather, King Edward VII, while he was Prince of Wales.

Janet Huse, Monarchy Canada Photo

On July 6, from the famous green podium of the General Assembly, Queen Elizabeth II spoke to the United Nations. Her Majesty praised the world organization as a "force for common good." The sovereign had addressed the UN, of which her sixteen realms are individual members, only once before — at the end of her Ottawa weekend in 1957.

A very relaxed queen and an equally at ease Stephen Harper, her prime minister, exchange comments at the Canada Day festivities.

The Canadian Press/Sean Kilpatrick

Chapter One

THE ROYAL FAMILY ARRIVES

1786–1789

(King William IV)

THE SEA HAS DETERMINED Canada's destiny. Most Canadians live thousands of kilometres inland and the sea is far from their minds. But it has never been far from their history or their wellbeing. The sea was what brought the explorers and the first European settlers. It was the Royal Navy's control of the sea and the St. Lawrence River that brought New France into British North America. It was the navy's temporary loss of that control to the European allies of the American rebels that led to the latter's victory at Yorktown, the creation of the United States and the exodus of the Loyalists to Canada, and the subsequent birth of an Anglo-French Canada. It was trade by sea that brought wealth to Canadians and the sea that brought immigrants to swell the population. And it was the sea that brought the royal family to Canada from 1786 through 1939.

In 1786 the Canada of today was but a dream in a few minds. The ancestors of most modern Canadians had never heard of Canada or, if they had, they were not contemplating it as the home of their children and descendants. There were the aboriginal peoples, who had lived on the continent for centuries; there were

fewer than one hundred thousand French Canadians; there were some British settlers in the Atlantic territories and newly arrived British entrepreneurs in Quebec City and Montreal; and the even more recently arrived Loyalist refugees from the American rebellion — perhaps 60,000 or more settling in the virgin forests of northern Nova Scotia and western Quebec, out of which they would create the provinces of New Brunswick and Ontario. And that was Canada.

But Canada was in the mind of the royal family. The king's third son, Prince William, an officer in the Royal Navy, had served in New York during the rebellion and in 1786, within three years of the arrival of the Loyalists, he arrived in Newfoundland and Nova Scotia, making Canada's royal family one of the earliest families to call the country its home.

Prince William was born in 1765 and began his naval career in 1779. He proved a good seaman and the king insisted that he earn his promotions by merit and not by his status, so he completed his full six years before promotion to lieutenant. He passed his examinations with ease. During those six years he had become a veteran of several battles.

The modern painting of Prince William (circa 1786), by artist Louise Topping, that is on display at the Castle Hill Museum in Placentia Bay.

A young Prince William, thirteen, was introduced into the Royal Navy in 1779 by his father, King George III (back towards viewer).

In 1781, he was assigned to HMS *Barfleur*, flagship of Admiral Hood, which sailed to New York, still in Loyalist hands after the fall of Yorktown earlier that year. William was allowed to engage in some sightseeing in the colonial town. A Colonel Ogden, on the staff of George Washington, received approval to attempt to kidnap the royal prince on one of his sojourns, so long as no harm or indignity came to him. However, nothing came of the intrigue.

The prince was subsequently assigned to the fifty-gun frigate HMS *Warwick*. While he was serving with her she captured the French forty-gun frigate *L'Aigle*, the twenty-seven-gun *Sapphire*, and the sloop *Terrier*. He was then assigned back to the *Barfleur*, and took part in operations in the West Indies into 1785, at which point he returned with her to England and then spent time touring Germany and Italy.

On April 10, 1786, William was given his first command, HMS *Pegasus*, a twenty-eight-gun frigate and the same ship that he had been appointed first lieutenant of the previous February. It was in command of that ship that the prince travelled to Newfoundland, Nova Scotia, and the then Province of Canada.

Returning to North America in 1786, he kept a detailed log of his experiences, which he illustrated with watercolour drawings. These records and the prince's letters to his father provide a unique look at life in early Canada from the perspective of a royal, but serving officer.

Prince William's first impressions of Newfoundland were not encouraging. On September 21 he wrote to the king:

> The face of the country is truly deplorable: the season as far backward as the beginning of April: a small brushwood for the first five hundred yards in shore and then a most dreadful inhospitable and barren country intersected by fresh water ponds, lakes and bogs: I am informed that the woods are very large thirty miles from the sea, and are a prodigious size and extent. Few people have ever visited the inland parts of the island so that

HMS Pegasus, *the ship that brought the first member of the royal family to Canada, depicted in this watercolour arriving in St. John's harbour, Newfoundland.*

This painting of Halifax harbour is attributed to Prince William.

they are scarce known; it is not even determined whether they are inhabited.

Soon after his arrival, the prince found himself involved in civil as well as naval affairs. At the time there were no permanent civil authorities in most of the province, so the visiting senior naval officer found himself in charge. In Placentia, Prince William had to break up a riot on one occasion and presided over a court on another. He also took a keen interest in the religious welfare of the community, including in his correspondence to the king an account of his activities:

Portrait of King William IV in the hallway outside the red chamber, Province House, Halifax, was sent to Nova Scotia by the king after his accession.

During the last fortnight of our stay at Placentia I read Divine Service in the courthouse for an example to the magistrates to perform that duty every Sunday till the arrival of the missionary from England. I twice led prayers and my congregation consisted of all the Protestants and many of the Catholicks [*sic*].

His interest went beyond conducting services. As Placentia's surrogate he commissioned the construction of a church, to which he personally contributed a significant sum. The church, St. Luke's, still stands today. In 1787 he sent the new house of worship silver communion plate consisting of a chalice and paten, a plate, and a flagon. These remain among the treasures of the Anglican Diocese of Eastern Newfoundland and Labrador.

The North America Station was based in Halifax and eventually the *Pegasus* proceeded to its main base, where the prince was received with royal ceremony. However, he made it clear that in the future he was to receive no special treatment not accorded to an officer of his rank. Prince William found Halifax, "A very gay and lively place full of women and those of the most obliging kind." Although he had just turned twenty-one, Prince William was already acquiring a reputation for inappropriate liaisons that would continue for much of his life.

The ships of the North America Station ranged as far south as the Caribbean, north to Newfoundland, and up the St. Lawrence River into Canada. In his year's assignment Prince William followed this pattern of service and was temporarily transferred to the Leeward Islands Station in the Caribbean. While there he met a naval captain of comparable age, Horatio Nelson, with whom he became close friends. Nelson's friendship and support of the prince lasted until the former's death in 1805 at the famous Battle of Trafalgar, by which time both men were admirals. Nelson said of his new colleague:

Our prince is a gallant man; he is indeed volatile but always with great good nature … He has his foibles as well as private men but

26

Frances Wentworth, wife of Sir John Wentworth, Bart, the governor of Nova Scotia 1792 to 1808, was reputed to be one of Prince William's many lovers.

the views in summer are magnificent, and where in England the eye commands a view of ten miles, in Canada for many leagues the corn and the sky appear to meet. The ground is rich and if the industrious Englishman tilled it instead of the lazy Canadian, it would be inestimable. The country about Quebec is vastly inferior in beauty and richness to that about Montreal. My time was too short this year to go higher up than Montreal, but next summer I shall most certainly proceed as far as possible.

The prince's view of French Canadians was not shared by his younger brother, Prince Edward, who was to establish very close relations with the new subjects of the king, and redress the bias of his brother, during his residence in Canada from 1791 to 1800. While in Canada, Prince William eventually travelled as far inland as modern-day Cornwall, Ontario, where he encouraged the Loyalist settlers creating a new home in the wilderness where they could continue to live in North America as subjects of the crown. The prince also had a favourable view of the Native people and their relationship to the crown, which he also conveyed to the king in his correspondence of October 9, 1787:

they are far out-balanced by his virtues. In his professional line he is superior to nearly two-thirds, I am sure, of the list; and in attention to orders and respect to his superior officers I know hardly his equal. HRH keeps up strict discipline in this ship, and without paying him any compliment she is one of the finest ordered frigates I have seen.

At Nelson's marriage on March 11, 1787, Prince William acted as the surrogate father of the bride.

Prince William's opinion of Quebec, then known simply as the Province of Canada, was much higher than his view of Newfoundland, notwithstanding his critical opinion of French Canadians, as indicated in another letter to his father, written on October 9, 1787.

As for the Province of Canada it vastly surpasses all the accounts I can give to Your Majesty of its magnitude, beauty and fertility: the Province in extent is larger than all Europe:

Near Mon[t]real the Indians begin to inhabit … The sensations they expressed at my visit were too strong not to be natural; their language was peculiarly pointed in saying they then saw one in whose veins flowed the same blood as in the body of their Great Father in the East, meaning Your Majesty; The Indians not only love your Majesty but they go further in adoring, their respect being so wonderfully great for every thing that relates to Your Majesty.

Although he was a stickler for protocol and discipline, the prince was not above violating the rules himself. While serving in the West Indies, and depressed after his friend Nelson's departure, he took his ship back to Halifax without permission. As a punishment he was ordered to winter in Quebec, but instead sailed back to England, arriving in Portsmouth in December. The king and the Admiralty were furious and William was ordered to remain within the limits of the port until he was sent back to Halifax in the following year.

As it turned out he was assigned to the Channel Squadron, but a love affair he had started in Plymouth was too much for his father, who made his views forcefully known, "What, William playing the fool again? Send him off to America and forbid the return of the ship to Plymouth." Prince William's naval career never really recovered from his indiscretions and breaches of discipline between 1787 and 1788.

The second posting of Prince William to the North America Station lasted for a year, and he left England in command of HMS *Andromeda*, a thirty-two-gun

ship, in July 1788. Maintaining his reputation as a firm disciplinarian, but one who looked after his men, in August he complained to the senior officer in Halifax that there was, "A quantity of bread, butter and cheese on board, which is mouldy, rotten and rancid and unfit for men to eat."

After his departure from North America in 1789, William did not return again. But his association with the new world did not end. In 1830 he succeeded his brother, King George IV, and reigned as King William IV from 1830 to 1837. As king he sent a picture of himself to the Nova Scotia Legislature, recalling his earlier life in the provincial capital.

In 1789, shortly after the prince returned to England from North America, he began a relationship with

King William IV's two daughters who came to Canada are seen in this family picture. Lady Mary Fitzclarence is the first on the left in profile, with back to viewer. She married Colonel Charles Richard Fox, who commanded the 34th Regiment of Foot in Nova Scotia in 1830. Lady Amelia Fitzclarence is fourth from the left. She was the wife of Lucius Cary, tenth Viscount Falkland, the governor of Nova Scotia from 1840 to 1846.

Confederation Life Collection

The Royal William, *built at Quebec and named after King William IV, was the first ship to cross the Atlantic Ocean under steam. It made the crossing in August 1833, taking twenty-five days.*

Dorothy Jordan, an Irish stage beauty. Unacceptable as a royal bride, she remained his common-law wife for the next twenty years and bore him ten children, readily acknowledged by their royal father, who gave them the surname of Fitzclarence, after his newly received title of Duke of Clarence, and he ensured good marriages and official status for them. From his marriage to Princess Adelaide of Saxe-Meiningen in 1818 he had two legitimate daughters who died as infants.

Two of his illegitimate daughters also went to Nova Scotia. Mary Fitzclarence became the wife of Colonel Charles Richard Fox who, as commanding officer of the 34th Regiment of Foot, was stationed in Nova Scotia in 1830 and was accompanied by his wife. Amelia Fitzclarence achieved an even higher position. She married Viscount Falkland, who served as governor of Nova Scotia from 1840–46 and thus, as Viscountess Falkland, she was the chatelaine of Government House in Halifax, the city where her father had spent many months of his naval career.

King William IV is also remembered in the geography of Canada with several places named after him, both during the time he was in Canada and later. These include: Prince William, New Brunswick (originally Prince William Township in 1783, and Prince William Parish in 1786); Williamsburg, Ontario, 1787; Clarenceville, Quebec, 1787; and King William Island,

Nunavut, 1830. As king he also gave the royal charters to Prince of Wales College, Charlottetown, and Victoria University, Toronto (as Upper Canada Academy), of which he is the royal founder, both in 1834.

Although the influence of King William IV on Canada during his stay as Prince William was not so great as that of members of the royal family who followed him, his residence established the essential principles that were to characterize the royal presence over the next centuries: Canada was a home for the royal family to live in and to serve in, not a foreign land to merely visit; the country was important enough to the royal family for the highest ranking members of the family to go there; and by participating in Canadian life in its varied form the royal family would be making Canada royal and themselves Canadian. And it started with a twenty-year-old sailor prince.

In Ottawa the Senate foyer includes an 1831 portrait engraving of King William IV by Frederick Christian Lewis, from an 1827 drawing by Sir Thomas Lawrence. The engraving was donated to the Parliament of Canada by Senator Serge Joyal.

29

Chapter Two

PRINCE AMONG PIONEERS

1791–1800

(Prince Edward, Duke of Kent)

MILITARY SERVICE BROUGHT His Royal Highness Prince Edward, second member of the royal family, to tour Canada. He arrived at Quebec City on August 11, 1791, five years after his elder brother, Prince William. He came as colonel of the Royal Fusiliers, 7th Regiment of Foot, bringing his unit with him to garrison Quebec.

With drums beating and instruments playing, the young commanding officer — he was not yet twenty-four — marched his men uphill from Lower Town into the fortress city the moment he stepped ashore. No speeches, guns, or ceremonies marked his entry, unlike the flamboyant advent of his brother five years before.

The tall — over six feet — well-built Prince Edward, blue eyed with blond hair and fair complexion, had recognizable Hanoverian features to identify him as King George III's son. He was dignified but affable, fluently French-speaking, and abstemious. The Quebec populace's first impression of him was favourable. As a regimental commander his position was minor. But he was the king's son. With the governor-in-chief, Lord Dorchester, preparing to take a two-year leave of absence, Edward was ideally placed to take centre stage.

Prince Edward was called on in his princely capacity almost at once. Forty Native chiefs, representing the Confederated Western Nations, arrived to complain to the governor general about American border incursions. Lord Dorchester seized the opportunity to present them to the prince. "Brothers! Here is Prince Edward, son of our king, who has just arrived with a chosen band of his warriors to protect this country," he announced. "I leave him second in command of all the king's warriors in Canada and he will take care of you."

The excitement of Prince Edward's arrival was not diminished as word flew around Quebec that he had not come alone. There was a mysterious lady with him. She was Thérèse-Bernardine Mongenet, a pretty French woman of middle-class origin, seven years his senior. To history she is known as "Madame de St. Laurent," to the prince and his circle "Julie," to his brothers "Edward's French lady," to others "Madame."

Julie was a recent acquisition. A lusty Hanoverian, Edward had realized, after a scrape involving an actress, that he needed stability. He instituted a discreet search for "a young lady to be my companion and mistress of my house." Madame de St. Laurent fit the bill. The

The young Prince Edward, later Duke of Kent, was colonel of the 7th Royal Fusiliers when he was posted to Quebec.

Thérèse-Bernardine de Mongenet, Prince Edward's "Julie," known in Canada as Madame de St. Laurent.

prince could hardly have chosen better. Julie was as elegant and well bred as she was sensible. Her English was perfect. She was good tempered and cheerful. Above all she was discreet. Everyone found the dark-haired, slender beauty with blue eyes, charming and vivacious. The prince adored her. Civilized if not moral, their mutual arrangement lasted twenty-eight years.

Prince Edward came to Quebec at a crucial period. The Constitutional Act passed that year at Westminster divided it into two provinces, Upper and Lower Canada. Against that background, His Royal Highness started out on his first Canadian tour the following summer. He left Quebec City on August 11, 1792, taking along his own curricle.

His route lay first by road to Montreal. The royal party travelled by calèche and drank in the beautiful St. Lawrence River scenery on the way. Though journeying in a "private capacity," as prince, Edward could not escape ceremonious welcomes. At the post house at Berthier, five militia captains, led by the seigneur, met His Royal Highness and his suite. They escorted him to the manor for "elegant entertainment." Twenty-one small cannon fired a salute. The bells of St. Cuthbert's Chapel rang throughout the visit.

From Montreal the royal party pressed on, alternating between calèche and batteau. At the Cascades, the rapids west of the junction of the Ottawa and St. Lawrence Rivers, the batteau was towed up the bank and passed through several locks. As they rowed along, the watermen sang softly, led by the helmsman in a minor key. At Ogdensburg a royal barge awaited the prince. It had been fitted by order of John Graves

Simcoe, lieutenant-governor of the new province of Upper Canada. Under awnings and sail, the newly painted barge threaded its leisurely way through the enchanting Thousand Islands.

For the two hundred mile voyage up Lake Ontario, the prince transferred to an eighty-ton armed topsail schooner, the *Onondaga*, at Kingston. He sailed past the pioneer Loyalist settlements on the north shore, in townships named for his brothers and sisters; past the harbour where the next year Simcoe would establish Toronto as the capital of Upper Canada. Prince Edward was assisting at the birth of Ontario.

When he reached Newark (Niagara-on-the-Lake), August 21, Prince Edward found the Simcoes living in three marquee tents. The only mishap of the tour occurred there. Determined to greet the prince "with every respect due to his illustrious birth" on his journey to see "the stupendous wonder of this country," the eager Simcoe stood too near the cannon firing the royal salute. The thundering explosion gave him a violent headache. "He was unable to see the prince after that day," his wife noted in her diary, "and kept his room for a fortnight."

On August 23, His Royal Highness crossed the river to review the troops at Fort Niagara. Though in

Meeting of Prince Edward and John Graves Simcoe, lieutenant-governor of Upper Canada, at the provincial capital, Newark (Niagara-on-the-Lake), August 21, 1792.

King Louis XIV Canadian Royal Heritage Archives

the United States, the stone French regime fort was still held by crown forces. History mentions no visit to Niagara Falls. Years later, however, the prince pointed out his old curricle to Mr. Justice George Hardinge with the words, "I was never split from it but once. It was in *Canada*, near the Falls of *Niagara*, over a concealed stump in a wood just cleared."

Another close encounter with the Native peoples, whom he had asked to see, greatly impressed His Royal Highness. He described it when writing to his father. "A very large deputation … of all the neighbouring nations came to Niagara to await my arrival … Their professions of attachment to your Majesty … were extremely warm."

Wherever the Prince went his presence gave assurance, hope, and cheer to the settlers. Summing up the tour, Prince Edward told George III, "I visited every post occupied by his Majesty's troops both in Upper & Lower Canada between Fort Erie & Quebec, excepting Oswego, which I was prevented from doing by a very violent storm which overtook us on Lake Ontario & render'd it entirely impossible to get ashore at that post."

Did Madame de St. Laurent accompany the prince to Montreal and Upper Canada? The records are silent. Given her subsequent practice of travelling with her royal lover, Mollie Gillen, their biographer, concludes she did. Because of her irregular position, Madame never appeared in an official capacity with the prince. There was no reason for her to be noticed.

Passing through Montreal on his way back to Quebec City, Prince Edward received an address from the citizens. He had left Upper Canada before Simcoe summoned its first Legislature. In Lower Canada, constitutional government got off the ground sooner, giving the prince his finest moment. Elections for the first assembly were held in May. Heated and bitter riding contests often divided on linguistic lines. Prince Edward was present at the Charlesbourg election as an observer. A treacherous attempt to close the poll and prevent electors from voting sparked his ire.

His Royal Highness sprang to the hustings. He addressed the angry crowd "in pure French, and with a tone of affection and authority." "Part then in peace," he entreated. "I urge you to unanimity and concord. Let me hear no more of the odious distinction of *English* and *French*. You are all His Britannick Majesty's *beloved* Canadian subjects."

Until then, Canadian meant Canadien, a native French speaker. With his words, Prince Edward redefined Canadian to include both English and French

In the election for Quebec's first assembly, which met in December 1792, Prince Edward personally quelled a polling riot. Painting of the assembly's first session by J.D. Kelly after C. Huot.

Kent House, rue St-Louis, Quebec, where Prince Edward and Madame de St. Laurent lived.

to Edouard-Alphonse de Salaberry in July 1792. The prince's proposal offering himself as sponsor caused a flutter among the Catholic clergy. But the latter tactfully acquiesced, reasoning that since the Anglican prince did not hold the baby he was not actually the godparent.

One day Edward received an invitation to dine at the Recollet Monastery from the Superior, Father de Berey, a former regimental chaplain. To honour his guest, the host fitted up a model artillery battery ready to fire a salute the moment the prince and his aides stepped through the door at noon. Unfortunately His Royal Highness was early. Edward, finding his host unaccountably annoyed, was amused when told why. He laughed even more heartily at dinner when, just as

Fine quality secretary desk made for Prince Edward in Quebec.

inhabitants of the country. He gave Canadian its modern meaning. Coming from the king's own son, the new sense of the word carried authority.

Prince Edward and Madame settled down to life in Quebec. They had a town residence in the rue St-Louis, Kent House, and a country place, Haldimand House, overlooking Montmorency Falls. Their social round consisted of dances, small dinner parties, theatricals, concerts, and winter picnics. The prince's excellent band supplied music for all of those events, but also for ordinary citizens and church services. Madame and the prince made many friends, especially the delightful de Salaberry family, and Catholic clergy such as Pierre-Louis Renaud, Curé of Beauport.

"Prince Edward makes this a lively place" commented an observer. In addition to routine military duties and visits to the de Salaberrys at their Beauport manor house, Edward fought fires in the city, attended masonic meetings, sponsored a Sunday school, assisted in creating an Anglican diocese, and quelled a planned mutiny in the garrison. He and Madame even acted as godparents

Father de Berey proposed his health, the forgotten guns suddenly exploded.

Edward visited a centenarian he'd heard of on the Île d'Orléans. Impressed by her clear mind, he asked the old lady if he could do anything for her. "Oh yes, Your Royal Highness," she replied. "Dance a minuet with me, so I may say before I die that I've had the honour of dancing with my sovereign's son." The prince gallantly obliged. Afterwards, he led her back to her chair and the dowager made him a deep curtsey.

One evening at Jean Natte's rue d'Aiguillon marionette theatre, His Royal Highness saw a reenactment of the 1775–76 American siege of Quebec. The performance highlighted the proper beating that the Americans had been given "so they'd learn to treat their neighbours with respect." As the show ended, "God Save the King" was played. Marionettes depicting the entire royal family paraded on stage. George III was mounted on a thoroughbred "with Queen Charlotte riding pillion on its wide rump." At the sight of his youngest brother, Prince Adolphus, Edward "broke down" and "hid his face in his handkerchief."

Prince Edward had not sought to come to Canada, duty brought him. Furious with his son for running up debts, the king's solution was to keep him abroad. Edward faced a dilemma. Lack of income to support his princely rank forced him to borrow money.

Canada was the back of beyond. Edward was always hoping to be recalled to the greater world, where events were moving fast as the French Revolution degenerated into terror, dictatorship, and world war. Congenial as Quebec life was, the prince and Madame found Canadian winters, even with their madcap frolics, bitter and long. Edward chaffed at his inactivity. In view of the isolation he felt it is a wonder he took so readily and genuinely to Canadians.

Letter from Prince Edward to Major-General Sir Alured Clarke, lieutenant-governor of Quebec, requesting that His Royal Highness's military band, which was not on strength, be given rations and fuel. It shows the prince's concern for his men.

Barbara Rusch

Garry Toffoli

Kent Gate in Quebec City was created as a memorial to Prince Edward by his daughter, Queen Victoria, in 1879. It was part of the sovereign's contribution to preservation of the city's ancient walls.

In 1793 France's declaration of war brought the opportunity for transfer. On Christmas Eve, Prince Edward received word of his promotion to major-general and orders to proceed to the West Indies. Eager to go, he still could honestly say in reply to addresses on departure, "I shall not leave Quebec without regret." The St. Lawrence River was frozen so his journey had to be overland, which was also the shortest route. The first member of the royal family to enter the newly formed United States would do so from Canada.

Through woodland trail and frozen river, the royal party moved slowly south by sleigh. At Lake Champlain they decided to chance the ice and cross to Burlington, Vermont. Though it looked solid, the surface had been weakened by a thaw. A horrified prince saw the two sleighs laden with the bulk of his plate, linen, and considerable library of books suddenly crack the surface, plunge through into the water, and sink to the bottom.

The royal party reached Portsmouth, New Hampshire, early in February. Proceeding on to Boston, the prince found he had to wait for the packet coming from Halifax to take him to Martinique. Americans, hostile to royalty because of the revolution, were divided into anti-British and anti-French factions on the war.

However, the reaction in Boston to the prince's prolonged unofficial royal presence was surprisingly warm. Edward received visitors and attended social events, creating excitement in the city. Loyalists, silenced by the revolution, emerged from the woodwork to show their approbation. Madame meanwhile sailed to Halifax and then to England.

On reaching the West Indies, Prince Edward showed his mettle in action. In the taking of Martinique, St. Lucia, and Guadeloupe he played a brave and key role. When the campaign ended the prince pressed on to Halifax aboard HMS *Blanche* to await the king's orders. He arrived there May 10, 1793, beginning his second Canadian sojourn.

Nova Scotia had entered a new era. With the arrival of 35,000 Loyalists its population had doubled, and part of its territory had been severed to create the province of New Brunswick. Edward spent two weeks getting acquainted with both provinces. Leaving June 14, he travelled overland to Annapolis. From there he crossed the Bay of Fundy to Saint John on the war sloop *Zebra*. He successfully risked running the falls at Saint John and impressed the New Brunswick solicitor general, Ward Chipman, who wrote of him as "the most accomplished character I have ever seen."

Edward half expected to return to Quebec. But the ship bringing Madame de St. Laurent back also carried his appointment as commander of the royal forces in Nova Scotia and New Brunswick. He made a home for himself and Madame in Halifax. A small country house called "Friar Lawrence's Cell" on Bedford Basin was lent him by the governor of Nova Scotia, Sir John Wentworth.

Sir John and Lady Wentworth openly received Madame, whom they liked. This recognition meant a much wider social life for the prince and his lady than at Quebec. Edward rebuilt the Wentworth country house as The Lodge, popularly called "Prince's Lodge," erected a rotunda for his band, which had arrived from

One of Prince Edward's major defence projects in the Maritimes was rebuilding the Halifax Citadel between 1796 and 1798. It was named Fort George after the prince's father, King George III.

cornerstones of the Round Church (St. George's), and Freemasons' Hall and was an early patron of the theatre. His example of building, both public and private, spurred the monied citizens to emulate him. By leaving parties early and getting up early, he reduced drunkenness among his officers. To cure the irritating unpunctuality of Haligonians, the prince gave the city its famous town clock, Halifax's most recognizable landmark, though it was not erected until 1803 after he left. Prince Edward even had his troops shovel out the Windsor Road whenever it was blocked by snowstorms.

On a fall afternoon in 1798, the prince was returning from a field day when his powerful horse slipped

Quebec, and laid out walks and gardens that were said to spell out the name "Julie."

Nova Scotians would look back on Prince Edward's Halifax years as a golden age. Through his restless activity and ability to obtain funds from London, His Royal Highness transformed the provincial capital. From a defenceless wooden town it slowly became a city with distinguished public and military buildings. Edward's work on its fortifications, including rebuilding the citadel, creating Martello towers, and replacing old installations on George's Island, made Halifax the strongest fortress outside Europe.

One of the prince's inventions was the first telegraph signal system in North America. It used a code of flags, large black and white balls, and drums by day and lanterns by night. The telegraph allowed fast communication with Annapolis, 130 miles away. Edward envisioned its expansion to Saint John, Fredericton, and Quebec. In the end it was completed as far as Fredericton, though the dense summer fogs in the Bay of Fundy hampered it. Edward's Camperdown signal station remained in operation until 1926.

The prince bought Navy Island at Halifax as a site for a hospital for infectious diseases. He laid the

St. George's Round Church, Halifax, a national historical site, was inspired by the Duke of Kent and built for German Lutherans. Edward, who contributed to the cost, may have chosen the unique design. The church is seen here during restoration after a devastating fire in 1994.

37

Public Archives of Nova Scotia

Arthur Bousfield

Top: *Ruins of Prince's Lodge, Bedford Basin, country residence of Prince Edward and Madame de St. Laurent.*

Bottom: *The rotunda for His Royal Highness's military band is the sole survivor of the estate buildings.*

on a Halifax street, throwing him and injuring his left thigh. A makeshift stretcher was needed to carry the hurt Edward home. His fall aggravated the rheumatism he already suffered from. When he did not recover, Dr. Mervin Nooth was summoned from Quebec. He prescribed the curative waters of Bath. Edward and Madame seized the opportunity to set sail and arrived in Portsmouth on November 14.

Edward made the most of his few months in England. He improved his dire finances. Able as he was, fiscal success eluded him. On March 11, 1799, parliament voted him the settlement — £12,000 a year — to which he had long been entitled. Another amendment to the neglect he felt was conferral of the royal Dukedoms of Kent and Strathearn and Earldom of Dublin on him. From then on he would be known as Duke of Kent. Finally, on the seventeeth of April he was appointed commander-in-chief of all the king's forces in North America.

Canadians were not remiss in expressing gratitude for all he had done for them. The Assembly of Saint

Halifax's best known landmark, the old town clock on Citadel Hill, was a gift to its citizens from the Duke of Kent in 1803.

John's Island resolved that their province be renamed Prince Edward Island, a resolution acted on by the king, February 5, 1799. Not to be outdone, the Nova Scotia House of Assembly voted an address of gratitude and five hundred guineas to purchase a Star of the Garter in diamonds for the duke. The star was ordered in July 1798 and duly presented to him at Kensington Palace.

Edward embarked in the summer for his third Canadian sojourn, arriving at Halifax on September 19, 1799. Commanders-in-chief had always made their headquarters in Quebec but the duke wisely decided his would be in Halifax, an ice-free port. Entering zestfully into his new duties he arranged that provincial volunteer corps could serve anywhere in North America, and planned an improved mail service between Halifax and Quebec.

The duke worked non-stop thirteen or fourteen hours a day, finding a secretary and five under-secretaries insufficient for all his business. Though his health began to suffer again, he planned new tours of Upper and Lower Canada, Prince Edward Island, Cape Breton, and Newfoundland for summer 1800 to inspect his whole command.

Despite those plans, the following year he broke the news to his friend de Salaberry that the king had given him permission to return to England, "for the

Prince Edward with native chiefs at Halifax about 1796.

C.W. Jefferys from a lithograph by H. Linch after a painting by H.D. Thielcke

Communications Nova Scotia

Prince Edward at Halifax, 1796, a painting by S. Weaver. The prince was a patron of the city's Theatre Royal, brought actor Charles Powell from England to be its manager and laid out one-way streets for playgoer rush hours.

present, on account of my lost health." Accompanied by Madame, he left Canada August 3, 1800. With the approaching union of Ireland and Great Britain Edward hoped to obtain the command of Ireland. Unfortunately, that hope proved vain.

When he left Canada, Edward was by no means certain that he would not be back and he remained commander-in-chief of North America until 1802. In his eagerness to depart, Kent probably did not think he would later regard his decade in Canada as the brightest and sunniest of his life.

The Nova Scotia governor and council summed up Edward's impact in its address deploring his departure. "To your benevolence" their memorial read, "the indigent have owed their support; the tradesmen and mechanics employment; and the industrious of every description the means of reaping the recompense of their skill and diligence."

In 1818, the Duke of Kent left Madame de St. Laurent to marry, in order to produce an heir to the throne. He and his bride, Princess Victoria of Saxe-Coburg-Saalfeld, are depicted on this card advertising "Owbridge's Lung Tonic For Coughs and Colds." Their only child became Queen Victoria.

Barbara Rusch

Kent had aspired to be Canada's viceroy. As early as 1796 he speculated "if it be my destiny to be one day Governor General of British North America." Though he did not succeed, the post of commander-in-chief that he held is one half of the office now officially entitled "Governor General and Commander-in-Chief of Canada." Kent never abandoned his efforts to obtain the viceregal appointment. In 1811 he sought it again and failed because of the jealousy of his brother, the Prince of Wales.

For the rest of his life, Kent's interest in Canada burned bright. What satisfaction he must have felt knowing his defences played their role in thwarting American invasion in 1812, actively or as deterrents. During the war, he was the energetic patron of a public fund for veterans of the conflict. Elated at his protégé Charles de Salaberry's spectacular victory over the Americans at Châteauguay in 1813, he helped secure proper recognition for the hero.

In 1814 the duke wrote Jonathan Sewell, secretary of the Executive Council of Lower Canada and at one time lead violinist of a small musical group that Kent had put together at Quebec, suggesting a federal union of the North American provinces. The letter was cited by the Fathers of Confederation half a century later. In 1815 Kent helped Joseph Bouchette publish his pioneering *Topographical Description of Lower Canada* in French and English. His last achievement, aptly, was to father Queen Victoria, the "Mother of Confederation."

Communications Nova Scotia

Miniature of Madame de St. Laurent in the Nova Scotia Archives. When the Duke of Kent separated from Madame, for the sake of duty, their unsanctified romance had lasted twenty-eight years. "Julie" died in Paris in 1830 in dignified obscurity.

Chapter Three

PRINCE OF CONFEDERATION

1860

(King Edward VII)

I N 1860, A SECOND Edward, the Prince of Wales, came to Canada, following in the footsteps of his grandfather, the Duke of Kent, but venturing further than the duke ever dreamed of. Albert Edward he was called — Bertie in the royal family — but when he was summoned to the throne he chose Edward as his reign name. It is convenient to call him that here.

His tour, replete with duties and royal formalities, was of lasting importance to Canada. With slight variations, it became the standard model for royal tours for a century. As for Edward himself, in his official biographer's view, "it would be hard to exaggerate the success of that journey or the impact which it made upon the Prince of Wales."

On May 14, 1859, the Canadian parliament — Upper and Lower Canada were reunited as the Province of Canada in 1841 — wound up its current session. Its final business was passing an address "To the Queen's Most Excellent Majesty," unanimously agreed to by both houses. It was moved in the assembly by the premier, George-Étienne Cartier, and formally petitioned Queen Victoria "to be present upon the occasion of the opening of the Victoria Bridge, [at Montreal], with

Your Majesty's Royal Consort, and such members of Your Majesty's August Family as it may graciously please Your Majesty to select to accompany you."

The address gave concrete expression to the crown's North American subjects yearning to glimpse their royal family. The desire was the natural legacy of Prince William's fleeting visits and the Duke of Kent's prolonged residences the previous century. Even more recent stays of William IV's "natural" daughters, on husbandly tours of duty, stimulated it. But it wasn't possible for the royal family to heed the call until Queen Victoria's children had grown up, depleted as the family was by George III's unexpectedly barren descendents.

A deputation carried Canada's by no means modest petition to London. With a European war underway, Queen Victoria did not want to risk leaving Westminster in the hands of the politicians. Victoria and Albert's eldest son and heir, the Prince of Wales, was having a difficult adolescence. A tour might help him. The queen accepted the Canadian invitation for her son.

Facing page: *The eighteen-year-old Albert Edward, Prince of Wales, at the time of his tour of Canada.*

John Ross Robertson Collection/Toronto Reference Library

Province of Canada's deputation to Queen Victoria, 1859. The Honourable Sir Henry Smith, (centre, seated) speaker of the assembly, presented to the queen parliament's unanimous resolution asking Her Majesty, Prince Albert the Prince Consort, and all the royal family to tour Canada.

The youthful Edward — he would celebrate his nineteenth birthday after the tour — came in the custody of a ponderous suite. His large royal party boasted a secretary of state, an Oxford Regius Professor of Medicine, the Lord Steward of the Queen's Household, the minister accredited to Washington, not to mention governors and equerries. They reached St. John's, Newfoundland, July 24, 1860, on the ninety-one-gun battleship HMS *Hero*. Fashionably dressed ladies fluttering "spotless handkerchiefs" hailed His Royal Highness when he stepped onto Queen's Wharf. It was an auspicious beginning, one very much to his taste.

The prince's Newfoundland reception set the pattern for all the provinces. He got to know it well.

Addresses, with replies by Edward, were presented at the St. John's levee in front of two hundred spectators. The prince's zest for the formal ball in his honour, where he danced with twelve different ladies, was great enough to detain him in the room until 3:00 a.m. The day after, the royal party attended a regatta on Quidi Vidi Lake.

Lucky enough to ride out to see the town "unattended," the prince paid visits to both its cathedrals, Anglican and Roman Catholic. Cabot, a magnificent Newfoundland dog, silver collared and appropriately named, was presented to him from the people of the province. Though rain spoiled outdoor events during the visit, it could not dampen popular enthusiasm for the heir to the throne.

The prince landing at Halifax, 1860.

From the start, Edward's affable demeanour and charming manner were a major asset. They took people by storm. The curly haired prince with the fresh complexion and pleasant smile went out of his way to meet expectations. It was a change for a young man regarded by his parents as a bit of a disappointment to be told by the lieutenant-governor of Newfoundland that the best land in the province went for a dollar an acre but huge sums changed hands for a single ticket to the royal ball.

45

Rainy weather bedeviled the royal tour throughout the Maritimes. It followed the prince all the way to Quebec City. Four day's sail took the *Hero* from St. John's to Halifax, August 2. Magnificent is an apt description of the Warden of the North's reception of its sovereign's son. Alive with memories of the prince's grandfather, the city pulled out the stops. In its excitement it even forgot to publish the daily newspapers. A keen rivalry sprang up. Each city on the tour strove to outdo the others in its welcome.

Prince of Wales's levée, Government House, Halifax.

While at Halifax, Edward steamed up Bedford Basin to visit the ruins of Prince's Lodge, the Duke of Kent's old country house. A special train took the royal party to Windsor and Hantsport. There the prince boarded HMS *Styx* to sail across the Bay of Fundy to Saint John, New Brunswick. It was night when he reached it. Next morning, August 3, surprised citizens found the prince awaiting *them*. The official reception took place at the dock. A procession escorted His Royal Highness to the grounds of the former Chipman residence where 5,000 school children sang God Save the Queen, with special verses. One began

> Hail! Prince of Brunswick's line,
> New Brunswick shall be thine,
> Firm has she been.

On August 4, the steamer *Forest Queen* took the royal party up river to Fredericton, through the grand scenery of the Saint John River Valley. Bells rang and guns fired as the entire population of the New Brunswick capital turned out to greet the Prince of Wales. Before returning to Saint John, he attended service at the cathedral and inaugurated a park. At the old Loyalist seaport he again boarded the *Styx* to sail back to Windsor.

Travelling by rail and horse-drawn carriage through the forest to Truro and Pictou, he found *Hero* waiting for him there. At Charlottetown, Prince Edward Island, Edward gained experience in coping with unforeseen mishaps. Few turned up for the levee. Why? The wrong time had been announced. A sudden downpour completely ruined the planned fireworks. After he left Charlottetown on August 9, the weather broke, letting the prince view the southern coast of the St. Lawrence. The royal squadron stood inshore as they rounded Cape Gaspé where "huge cliffs of red sandstone lit up by the sun, seemed like mountains of fire."

The royal party sighted Percé Rock and entered Gaspé Basin. The governor general, Sir Edmund Head, and the co-premiers, George Etienne Cartier and John A. Macdonald, came on board to welcome the Prince of Wales to Canada. *Hero* then left for the Saguenay. From Tadousac, the prince went upstream to the junction of the Saguenay and St. Marguerite Rivers where he successfully fished for trout.

Arrival of the royal squadron carrying the Prince of Wales at Quebec.

August 17, *Hero* reached the Île d'Orléans. At Quebec City the prince made his public entry to Canada. The heights were dotted with people and the sun broke through as His Royal Highness arrived by barge from the ship. In the ancient city of French chevaliers, Edward knighted the speakers of the Legislative Council and Assembly, Narcisse Belleau and Henry Smith. For the illumination in his honour, at night even the humblest homes placed dip candles in their windows.

Sightseeing included a jaunt to Montmorency Falls. When His Royal Highness visited the famous Ursuline Convent on August 22, "the young lady pupils sang, with harp accompaniment, an ode composed for the occasion." At Laval University the loyal address presented to the prince described the institution as "the first and only French Canadian university thus honoured with the royal protection."

The prince pressed on to Montreal for the first of the tour's two major events, the opening of the Victoria Tubular Bridge. At Trois-Rivières, the steamer *Quebec*, with the members of parliament aboard, asked to join the royal escort. The peal and clang of bells in every community moved them along up river.

Montreal, Canada's largest city at the time with 90,000 people, had been in a frenzy of preparation. Two thousand dollars was spent on the embellishment of Viger Square, ten thousand on general celebrations, a provincial grant of twenty thousand went to a great exhibition, and public subscription money transformed the city. Houses were whitewashed, trees planted, fountains created, and ermine trimmed scarlet robes with a cocked hat, sword, and chain were bought for the mayor.

Torrential rain delayed Edward's entry until 1:30 p.m., August 25. But when his specially built open railway car drew in at Point St. Charles, the sun shone. Under a crimson canopy fringed with gold lace and furnished with handsome carpets, the prince saw the six-ton last stone of Victoria Bridge lowered into place. He tapped it a few times with a silver trowel. Next he went to the centre arch of the great span where he drove home the last — and silver — rivet with a large, heavy hammer.

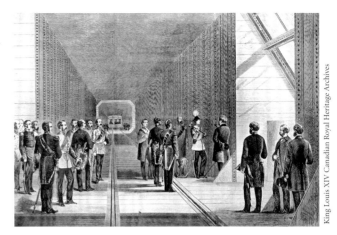

King Louis XIV Canadian Royal Heritage Archives

His Royal Highness drove in the last rivet of the Victoria Tubular Bridge, Montreal, one of the engineering wonder of the day in Canada, August 25, 1860.

Trowel with beaver handle and decorated with maple leaves used by the prince in laying the last stone of the bridge.

Specially built open train car used by the Prince of Wales and his party at the opening of the Victoria Bridge, Montreal.

The 1860 tour gave official recognition to the modern era in Canada — the age of the locomotive. But trains were still in their infancy. To save time, passengers often had to help the crew load fresh wood into the tender. But they were there to stay. Edward made as much use of them during the long journey as he could.

"Canada now possesses a complete system of railway communication," the directors of the Grand Trunk Railway noted in their royal address. In reply, the prince called the new railway bridge, on which construction began in 1854 and cost fifteen million dollars, "a work as unsurpassed by the grandeur of Egypt or of Rome, as it is unrivalled by the inventive genius of these days of ever-active genius." At the luncheon for seven hundred people that followed, Edward's toast was "Prosperity to Canada."

Montreal won the royal tour city rivalry hands down. Though the decorations had been battered by rain, its illumination was not by candlelight but gas. The city also saw *two* balls for the prince. One was the

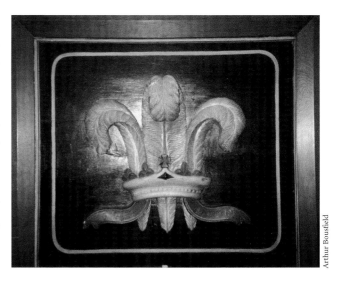

Surviving train car panel with Prince's badge.

grandest ball ever held in Canada. A wooden pavilion was built at the foot of Mount Royal for the occasion. A contemporary description had its fountains running with rose water, eau de cologne, and lavender. Read champagne and claret instead! The prince danced until 5:00 a.m., not sitting out once.

The city kept him busy, but Edward was so vital that despite being overtired he never flagged — unlike members of his suite who were seen dozing off at one dinner. For his five days in Montreal, Edward made Rosemount, residence of the commissioner of Public Works, his home. The prince also inaugurated the city's Crystal Palace, recalling the favourable impression made by the Province of Canada's exhibits at the Great Exhibition of 1851 in London.

From commercial capital to political, the Prince of Wales moved on to Ottawa. The journey alternated by train and Ottawa River steamer. As the royal party drew near on August 31, a red glow appeared to move over the water towards the steamer *Phoenix*. A flotilla of 150 lumbermen and Native canoes, their crews colourfully painted and befeathered or clad in red shirts, had come to meet and escort them to the city.

The Prince of Wales's visit was Ottawa's first major event. Eleven years before, in 1849, the Montreal populace disgraced itself by burning the parliament buildings in their city. In the interval, Kingston, Quebec, and Toronto had had turns as capital. The politicians

King Louis XIV Canadian Royal Heritage Archives

The prince laid the cornerstone of the parliament buildings of Canada, Ottawa.

King Louis XIV Canadian Royal Heritage Archives

Fireworks during the Prince of Wales's stay in Montreal. Attempting to view them incognito, the prince and his carriage were stopped by an officious policeman who refused to believe their identity and they had to retreat.

could not decide on a permanent site. Each parliamentarian had to advocate his own city for the role or risk electoral defeat.

To get the politicians off the hook, parliament asked Queen Victoria to choose the capital. In 1857 Her Majesty, to the dismay of many, selected the shanty lumberman's town of Ottawa, straddling the border between French and English Canada.

Arches, flags, and banners decorated the city. In reply to the corporation's address Edward broached the second purpose of his tour. "I am about to lay the first stone of a building in which, before long, the deliberations of the Parliament of Canada will be held; and from which will emanate the laws which are to

Cornerstone laid by the prince. After the fire of 1916 it was re-laid for the new parliament buildings by his brother, His Royal Highness the Duke of Connaught, governor general of Canada.

govern the great and free people of these provinces." Rain cut short the civic welcome. A procession hastily formed with "nearly the entire population" escorted His Royal Highness to Victoria House, the hotel leased as his temporary home.

Construction of the parliament buildings was well underway. The Gothic style of architecture had been chosen to proclaim the royal roots of Canada's constitutional practice in medieval times. It was to be a sharp contrast to the classical buildings of republican Washington, D.C., since Gothic was inspired by the forests of northern Europe, it would suit Canada.

The next morning, soon after 11:00, Edward arrived on Parliament Hill, as the site soon would be known. The Reverend Dr. Anderson, chaplain for the occasion, prayed that the completed building would be "used for the good of the province, the glory of our queen, the happiness of our prince, and the good government of our people." Once the stone was in place, the prince gave the finishing touches to the mortar with a silver trowel. Wags derided the wording on the corner stone. It referred, they said, to "the building *intended* to receive the Legislature of Canada." The ashes of the capital debate still smouldered. Five years would pass before the government moved in.

Edward drove to the Chaudière Falls where the thrilling experience of shooting down a timber slide awaited him. Afterward, he was rowed on the waters of the Ottawa River, where he watched a canoe regatta. The following day was Sunday so the Prince of Wales attended church. He also viewed a certain stone mansion built by Thomas Mackay, now called Rideau Hall. Before any governor general lived in it the house was familiar to the heir to the throne.

On Monday the Prince of Wales took his leave of Ottawa by water on the steamer *Emerald*. From Arnprior the royal party took carriages to Almonte, where they entrained for Brockville. Little did they know that a storm was brewing. Enraged by the Prince of Wales' courtesies to Catholics in the Maritimes and French Canada, the powerful Orange Order began erecting arches with anti-papal slogans along roads His Royal Highness would travel and laid plans to join processions in full regalia.

With royal standard flying, the prince and royal party experienced the thrill of the timber slide at the Chaudière Falls, Ottawa.

The situation came to a head in Kingston. The royal party arrived there on the steamer *Kingston* on September 4. From the deck they beheld two thousand angry Orangemen assembled on the quay, waving banners and shouting slogans. Edward's guardian, the Duke of Newcastle, Undersecretary of State for the Colonies, took charge. He went ashore to inform the mayor that the prince would not land unless the anti-Catholic demonstrators were dispersed, their arches removed. The mayor refused.

Right: *Photograph of Albert Edward, Prince of Wales at the time of his great Canadian tour.*

Arrival of the Kingston *(left, flying royal standard) at Toronto Harbour with His Royal Highness on board.*

National Gallery of Canada

Newcastle gave them overnight to reconsider. In the morning the *Kingston* sailed on to Belleville. Packed with farmers from the surrounding area who had come to see the prince, Belleville had two Orange arches without party emblems. But overnight the arches were hung with offensive material. Orangemen in full regalia paraded the streets. To the bitter disappointment of the city's people, *Kingston* sailed past them too.

Cobourg, the next town, had no demonstrators. The prince landed. His carriage was drawn by a new society called Native Canadians, with "silver maple-leaves on their breasts, who carried lighted torches." Edward opened a ball at 11:00 p.m. and danced until daylight with fifteen ladies.

Proceeding by train to Rice Lake, the royal party declined crossing the water by the dilapidated railway bridge (it collapsed not long after). They took the steamer *Otonabee*. A stop to receive greetings from the Mississaugas preceded Edward's arrival in Peterborough. Escorted in carriages to the courthouse, the prince accepted addresses from the corporation. It was at Peterborough that a man "with an enormous amount of brass" stretched out his brawny hand to shake hands with His Royal Highness. The friendly prince graciously complied, only to find he had opened the flood gates.

At Port Hope, Edward rejoined the *Kingston* to sail on to Toronto. The Orangemen of Toronto agreed to put aside their insignia. The mayor asked some Catholics to see if the one Orange arch was decorated with any objectionable matter. They said no.

The *Kingston* sailed into Toronto Harbour on September 7. Edward disembarked to a welcome that rivalled Montreal's. Seeing the Orange arch with a figure of King William III on it, Newcastle felt he had been deceived. He cancelled the invitations of the mayor and corporation to the prince's levee. The mayor and aldermen apologized and on September 11 the prince held a special levee for them, at which he also received Kingston and Belleville deputations tendering apologies. Newcastle's clumsy handling of this delicate crisis was widely criticized

On September 10, the Prince of Wales went by the Northern Railway on a day's excursion to Collingwood. On the way back addresses were received at Newmarket, Aurora, Bradford, and Barrie. September 11, back in Toronto, His Royal Highness attended the Royal Canadian Yacht Club's Regatta and agreed to become their Patron. He opened Queen's Park for the public, the site of the present legislature, and the Botanical Gardens (now Allan Gardens) where he planted a maple tree. All of Toronto's venerable figures met their prince. Bishop Strachan preached to him, Colonel Denison received his congratulations on the Toronto Volunteer Corps; Dr. Ryerson had 450 teachers sing "Hurrah for Canada" to him at the Educational Department.

The ball at Toronto's Crystal Palace, where Edward had twenty-one dance partners, was "all that could be desired." (Unlike in the United States, where the prince later complained of being forced to dance with the matrons instead of their pretty young daughters.) Leaving the city on September 12, His Royal Highness set out for London, visiting Guelph, Petersburg, and Stratford on the way. Tecumseh House was set aside as his headquarters in London. Again and again he had to appear at the window to acknowledge cheers of the citizens. London staged a splendid fireman's torchlight procession.

After London came the Native gathering at Sarnia. One hundred and fifty representatives of all tribes in the province came to show their devotion. An Ojibwa chief addressed Edward. "Great Brother," he said, "when you were a little child, your parents told you that there were such people as Indians in Canada; and now, since you have come to Canada yourself, you see them." To mark the day, the prince presented many

Receiving greetings from chiefs at the great gathering of the native peoples held to meet the prince at Sarnia.

large medals bearing the Queen's image. He noticed an outstanding young Mohawk, Oronhyatekha, whom he arranged to have study medicine at Oxford. The Native chief translator, Henry Pahtahquahong Chase, was singled out too. Years later he was received by the prince in London.

Edward returned to the Forest City for a ball at Tecumseh House. September 14, the royal party left for Niagara, stopping en route at Woodstock and Paris. At the latter, Edward transferred from the Great Western to the Buffalo and Lake Huron Railway, "which had also built a splendid state-car for the occasion." There was a stop to receive an address at Brantford. At Fort Erie, the royal party took the steamer *Clifton* to Chippawa, where they spent the night. In the evening, the prince went to view Niagara Falls, lit by fires along the cliffs

King Louis XIV Canadian Royal Heritage Archives

The prince saw Niagara Falls from table rock at the foot of the great cataract.

and with Bengal lights, a kind of firework used at sea that gives off a blue flame.

For the prince the most memorable experience at Niagara was watching the short muscular French acrobat, Charles Blondin, walk across the Horseshoe Falls on a tightrope, on September 15. Blondin performed the feat wheeling a man in a barrow. Duly impressed, His Royal Highness gave him a purse of gold coins worth $400. Blondin, quick to seize an opportunity, offered to wheel the prince back across the cataract. The high-spirited Edward accepted. Advisers hastily intervened to stop him. Blondin crossed back to the United States unaccompanied — on stilts.

The Prince of Wales did go to the American side but by open ferry boat. He received an address on the Suspension Bridge, getting a magnificent view of the falls from the centre. A ride in the country towards the

Welland Canal showed him the fertile farming countryside of the peninsula. At Queenston, September 18, His Royal Highness greeted 160 survivors of the War of 1812, including the heroine Laura Secord. There he laid the foundation stone of a monument to the Saviour of Upper Canada, Major-General Sir Isaac Brock.

Edward's eloquent words offered a civilized definition of patriotism. "I have willingly consented to lay the first stone of this monument," he said. "Every nation may, without offence to its neighbours, commemorate its heroes, their deeds of arms, and their noble deaths. This is no taunting boast of victory, no revival of long-passed animosities, but a noble tribute to a soldier's fame; the more honourable, because we readily acknowledge the bravery and chivalry of that people by whose hands he fell."

At Niagara-on-the-Lake, the prince found that one of the welcoming arches bore the date of his grandfather's arrival there in 1792. Gifts of local fresh fruit were accepted. Port Dalhousie, St. Catharines, and Grimsby brought the royal party to Hamilton. The prince paid a private visit to the city's Crystal Palace before going again to officially open the Agricultural Society of Upper Canada's fifteenth exhibition.

Edward opened the city's water works on Burlington Beach outside the city. He also inaugurated Canada's first public room built as an art gallery. Only a prince with so great a natural appetite for pleasure could have endured another grand ball, for Hamilton held one for the Prince of Wales, where, as was his rule, he danced every dance.

Bidding goodbye to the governor general and Canadian ministry at Windsor, Edward, emulating his grandfather sixty-six years before, crossed into the United States. Though he was incognito as Lord Renfrew, a "student," Americans welcomed him — 30,000 on his entry at Detroit — as the son of Queen Victoria. His month travelling in their country was a personal conquest.

When he left from Portland, Maine, on October 20, the Canadian premiers and cabinet members journeyed to see him off. The provinces of British North America were self-governing in important matters. Their cabinets depended on majorities in their elected

King Louis XIV Canadian Royal Heritage Archives

Hamilton's Crystal Palace, which His Royal Highness opened September 20, 1860, contained Canada's first public art gallery.

Rex Woods /Confederation Life Collection

The Prince of Wales's tour accelerated Confederation. Within six years Queen Victoria, attended by her daughter Princess Louise, received Sir John A. Macdonald in private audience on February 27, 1867, the day after the British North America Bill creating the Dominion of Canada was introduced into the House of Commons at Westminster.

assemblies. Neighbouring provinces were separate entities, often rivals. The first motion in the New Brunswick Assembly to invite the prince to tour was defeated. In the debate, members attacked the Province of Canada for taking the initiative in the matter.

The unparalleled interest and publicity surrounding Edward's tour focused attention on the common allegiance of all provinces to their queen. One of the addresses received by the prince in Montreal was from the inhabitants of the Red River Settlement in far off Manitoba. Many saw they had more in common than divided them. In the Maritimes especially the tour broke through rampant sectionalism.

Though none of the addresses the prince received mentioned union, within seven years of Edward's royal progress, the situation had completely changed. Two of those provinces, Nova Scotia and New Brunswick, were federated with the third, Canada, as the Dominion of Canada. A fourth, Manitoba, a fifth, British Columbia, and a sixth, Prince Edward Island, were soon to join them. Some credit goes to the Prince of Wales.

One important convert to the Confederation movement made by the tour was the Duke of Newcastle, Edward's officious minister in attendance. By bringing household china decorated with maple leaves with him, and in other ways, Edward encouraged the growth of a Canadian nationality. The 1860 tour helped the prince mature and become better equipped to be monarch, and it also created the desire for union among the people who saw him.

Sir John Macdonald and the other Fathers of Confederation were soon in London seeing the British North America Act through the Westminster parliament. When Queen Victoria congratulated her Canadian prime minister on showing so much loyalty, Macdonald spoke some carefully memorized words to her. "We have desired," he said, "in this measure [Confederation] to declare in the most solemn and emphatic manner our resolve to be under the sovereignty of Your Majesty and your family forever."

Chapter Four

PRINCESS ON THE RIDEAU

1878–1883

(Princess Louise, Duchess of Argyll)

THE PRINCE OF WALES'S triumphant, unifying 1860 tour opened the gates of Canada to Queen Victoria's children. In a year, Albert Edward — King Edward VII to be — was followed by his next brother, Prince Alfred, Duke of Edinburgh. Making a career in the Royal Navy, the industrious Alfred was posted to Halifax in 1861. In 1869, another of the Queen's sons, Prince Arthur, was on his way to Montreal with his regiment.

To have a royal family member actually *live* in Canada again was Benjamin Disraeli's inspiration. A romantic royalist, the visionary British prime minister understood how much this would please the people of the newly confederated country. Princess Louise, the queen's third daughter, and her husband of seven years, John Campbell, Marquis of Lorne, were the royalties he proposed; a young couple for a young country. The idea had possibilities. Disraeli's affectionate rapport with the queen allayed whatever doubts, and they were few, Her Majesty had about the scheme.

A rough early winter Atlantic voyage brought the newly appointed viceregal couple to Halifax, November 23, 1878. Princess Louise, horribly seasick on the journey, found a family member already in Canada. Now a naval commander at the fortress seaport, Prince Alfred was the first to greet his sister and her husband. With pageantry, colour, and traditional legalities, Lorne was sworn as governor general at Province House. He and the princess then left for Ottawa.

Their arrival at the capital in a rainstorm on December 2 plunged them into the ups and downs of Canadian life. Enraptured at having the heir of the Campbell chief in their midst, inventive well-wishers reworked the famous clan song to meet the occasion:

The Campbells are comin', hurrah, hurrah,
The Marquis of Lorne, the princess an' a'.
The Campbells are comin', hurrah, hurrah,
They come to a land that has won some renown,
A people most loyal to queen and the crown,
They come to hold court at fair Ottawa,
The Campbells are comin' hurrah, hurrah.

But the head of the ministry, Sir John A. Macdonald, who ought to have been at the arrival ceremony, was

King Louis XIV Canadian Royal Heritage Archives

Archives Canada

Left top: *Her Royal Highness Princess Louise. From a photograph by W. J. Topley, Ottawa.*

Left bottom: *A Halifax welcome. Princess Louise received a bouquet on landing at Halifax, November 23, 1878.*

Above: *The Marquis of Lorne as governor general.*

King Louis XIV Canadian Royal Heritage Archives

not. The most famous Father of Confederation was on an alcoholic binge. His absence allowed the Liberal opposition, scenting blood, to pretend he purposely insulted the princess.

Enthusiasm and the missing prime minister epitomized the Canada that Lorne and his princess had arrived in. Loyal it was but not wholly civilized. Lorne would never have been considered a suitable Canadian viceroy but for being the Queen's son-in-law. Prior to his appointment he was virtually unknown, without any concrete record of public service. The attraction of the appointment was having Louise in Canada. "The princess is winning all hearts," Sir Charles Tupper reported happily a few days after their arrival. According to His

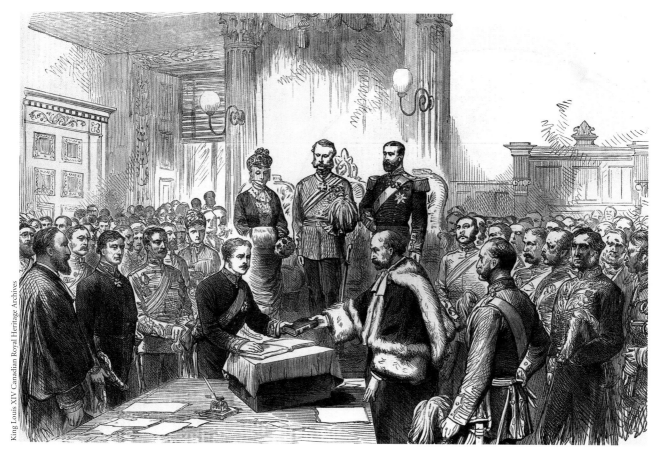

King Louis XIV Canadian Royal Heritage Archives

Lorne took his oath as governor general of Canada at Province House, Halifax, with Princess Louise and her brother Prince Alfred, Duke of Edinburgh looking on.

Excellency's secretary, "To see the daughter of the queen is the general wish of every inhabitant of Canada."

They were an attractive, energetic pair. Handsome, shortish, and of slim build, Ian Campbell, who had already travelled in Canada in 1866, was endowed with a fair complexion, bright blue eyes, and a wreath of golden hair. He spoke in a rather high-pitched nasal voice. Though a cheery man with an easygoing attitude, he was in no sense a personality. Indeed he was shy, modest, self-effacing, and at times stubborn. His marriage in 1871 to Queen Victoria's daughter had been a reversal of the monarch's marriage policy for her family. Since the sixteenth century children of the sovereign had married into royal or princely families. Victoria found that her first three daughters' marriages to princes took them from home. That was not what she wanted. To avoid it, she decided she did not mind after all if they married one of her subjects — a

suitable one of course. Lorne's and Louise's union was popular. Incorrigibly, the press toyed with the phrase "the maiden all for Lorne" in reporting it.

Princess Louise Caroline Alberta was the one beauty among the Queen's five daughters. She was also unique in having genuine artistic talent and with it the artistic temperament. Three years younger and somewhat taller than her husband, the princess was fair like him with long large blue eyes. Her features were regular. Bright, lively, critical, and mischievous, she possessed a deep voice and a loud whooping laugh. Though shy and likeable, she had no special charm. She was at her best helping people in trouble. At Rideau Hall she nursed people stricken down with scarlet fever when the servants would not go near them. To Louise's disappointment, her marriage, a love match, was childless.

The Lornes's time in office representing Queen Victoria turned out to be years of adventure and

On their way to Ottawa, the viceregal couple attended a ball given by the St. Andrew's Society. Before being escorted by pipers to supper, Lord Lorne took part in a Scottish reel.

adversity. They gave an impetus to Canada's growth and laid the foundations of institutions that are still important to arts and letters in the country.

After settling in at Ottawa, the Lornes's first excursion was not official but private. They made a trip to Niagara Falls in January 1879, travelling incognito as "Lord and Lady Sundridge," a disguise that fooled no one. The governor general opened his first parliament February 13. Later he and Princess Louise held a state drawing room in the senate chamber. At their first ball, some of the excited guests overindulged in champagne punch. A tipsy senator, finding Louise's train in the way, kicked it roughly aside.

From mid May the viceregal pair began their official tours to acquaint themselves with Canada. They went to Montreal for the queen's birthday, May 24, where the marquis knighted five prominent Canadians. At Kingston, the princess distributed prizes to Royal Military College cadets. In Quebec City, which both quickly grew to love, Lorne opened the Dufferin Terrace promenade on June 9, and Her Royal Highness laid the cornerstone of Kent Gate, Queen Victoria's gift to the city in memory of her father, the Duke of Kent. A private holiday followed. Making use of an old horse-drawn scow, converted into a houseboat and humorously named Great Caesar's Ghost, the princess and Lorne proceeded up the Restigouche River to Brandy Brook on a fishing expedition. Sometimes knee deep in water with her rod, Louise caught a twenty-eight-pound salmon.

The governor general and princess soon resumed their duties with a tour of the Maritimes. The parades, torchlight processions, arches, bunting, and flags that welcomed them in New Brunswick, Nova Scotia, and Prince Edward Island were the biggest since 1860. "It was undoubtedly the flesh and blood of a royal

Illustrated London News

Entry into Ottawa 1878.

John Evans

Door to Princess Louise's boudoir at Rideau Hall, hand-decorated by Her Royal Highness.

princess that sparked the extraordinary greeting," Robert Stamp rightly concludes in his *Royal Rebels: Princess Louise & the Marquis of Lorne.*

In Ontario, Lorne spoke German in Berlin (Kitchener) to the delighted approval of its Teutonic citizens. He opened the first Canadian National Exhibition in Toronto and his success raised the ire of Goldwyn Smith, a republican intellectual recently exported by Britain. Describing with a certain relish the formal presentations to the governor general and his lady in the Queen City, Alexander Mackenzie, leader of the opposition, wrote, "Lady Howland went through in grand style curtseying so low that everyone wondered how the whole of that 300 pound woman ever got up again."

When a somewhat homesick Princess Louise left Ottawa, October 18, to visit the queen in England, her first year in Canada was deemed a success. Louise

liked Canadians. She had done well. Sensible boots for walking, learning to skate, and warm furs made the winter less of a trial than she expected. The Canadian landscape provided endless subjects for sketching and painting. Louise even had an outdoor sketching box built for her and decorated the doors of her boudoir at Rideau Hall with graceful crab-apple branches that are still there. An initial fuss over etiquette, court dress, and proper clothes was overcome by common sense. "I wouldn't care if they came in blankets," exclaimed the amused princess about controversy over her Rideau

61

Hall guests' attire. In the capital, Louise dropped into shops unannounced. Her graciousness and thoughtfulness disarmed everybody. Her husband and an aide helped a distressed wagon driver replace a wheel. In short, the pair took the wind out of the sails of the "they're royalty, they must be snobs" critics.

The princess returned to the capital on February 3, 1880. In the twinkling of an eye things turned tragic. On February 14, the Lornes's horse-drawn sleigh set out from Rideau Hall for the first drawing room of the year at the senate. Taking the icy drive, it went too fast and slewed to the right. The horses bolted, the sleigh turned on its side. It was dragged 350 metres. Inside, Louise was thrown on top of her husband, pinning him down helpless. She hit her head on the metal framework of the sleigh. Her earring was wrenched out of her left ear and half the lobe torn away. Covered in blood, she managed to hold the head of her lady-in-waiting, Eva Langham, off the ground, saving her life.

"Louise has been much hurt, and it is a wonder her skull was not fractured," Lorne explained to Queen Victoria. "The muscles of her neck, shoulder and back are much strained." Instead of letting the public know the seriousness of the accident, Major de Winton, Lorne's secretary, panicked and played down the injuries to the press. As a result, the public got the idea the princess's injuries were trifling in nature. They were not.

Princess Louise had agonizing headaches and neuralgia in her face. It was a long time before she could sleep without medication. Months after her injuries appeared to have healed, she suffered from shock and was subject to sudden outbursts of rapid speech. The accident may have caused a slipped disk. When her brother, Prince Leopold, Queen Victoria's youngest and hemophilic son, arrived to stay at Rideau Hall in May, his tutor found Louise "unstrung and restless."

Louise did not appear in public again until April. She was still feeling too unwell to resume her official duties so she decided to travel with her brother. Together they went to Quebec, Toronto, and Niagara and spent ten days in Chicago. Identifying them easily, American journalists cheekily dubbed the royal sister and brother "Vic's Chicks." On their return to Canada, Louise and Leopold made a fishing expedition to Cascapedia.

When Prince Leopold returned to the United Kingdom on July 31, Princess Louise went with him. She did not come back to Canada until June 4, 1882. Much of the intervening time was spent in pursuit of restored health in England, Germany, France, and Italy. Ignorant of the real story of her injuries, the Canadian public was suspicious. Rumours propagated by the press suggested that Louise did not like the country or its people; that she had quarrelled with Lorne. Even wilder allegations such as having gone away to have a baby of whom Lorne was not the father were shamelessly spread.

Princess Louise missed her husband's most spectacular Canadian tour. In 1881, Lorne became the first governor general to visit the North-West Territory, that immense unsettled region of Canada between Manitoba and British Columbia. He got the Macdonald ministry to name part of the region Alberta in honour of his wife. (It was Princess Louise who chose the name of the Saskatchewan capital, Regina being the Latin word for queen.) Now Lorne hoped to promote immigration so that Canada would become a transcontinental reality and a power.

He left Toronto by rail, July 19, 1881. The steamer *Frances Smith* took the viceregal party from Owen Sound to Prince Arthur's Landing on Thunder Bay. Wabigoon Lake was the end of the railway and the journey from there was by steamer, barge, canoe, and strenuous portages. Winnipeg was "in a fever" to see the governor general. At Portage la Prairie, Lorne's party left the railway and struck off northwest. Travelling fifty or sixty kilometres a day with twenty-seven men, ninety-six horses, twenty-seven vehicles, and twenty-one tents, they reached Battleford on September 1. "Plateaux, hollows, ridges, and plains lie beneath you, on and on," wrote an awed Lorne of the terrain. "There is nothing to keep the eye and mind from the sense of an infinite vastness."

With the Cree chief Poundmaker as guide and a North West Mounted Police escort, the trek to Fort Calgary took two weeks. The party chased a herd of

Archives Canada

Meeting of Marquis of Lorne and Blackfoot tribe at Blackfoot Crossing on the Bow River, September 9, 1881, on the governor general's great tour of the west.

buffalo, killing several, in one of the last such hunts in Canadian history. Hardships multiplied as horses died, carts broke down, mosquitoes swarmed, prairie wolves howled. On September 9, at the Bow River, Chief Crowfoot and two hundred Blackfoot greeted "the Great Brother-in-Law," as the tribes called Lorne, just as Queen Victoria was known to them as the "Great White Mother." After pipe smoking and Native dances, Lorne heard the Blackfoot tell of loss of land and buffalo. In reply he told them the old days were gone. They should engage in agriculture. Crowfoot promised to "be the first in working."

The governor general was entranced by the beauty of the Rockies and southern Alberta, basking in lovely September weather. He reached Fort Calgary on September 12. His return route — after a council with the Bloods, another tribe of the Blackfoot Confederacy — was via Fort Shaw, Montana, and the Union Pacific Railway. On the way, he made a detour to Winnipeg to tell the Manitoba Club and a bevy of Canadian and

Looking towards the Rocky Mountains near Fort Calgary, an engraving of a drawing by the Marquis of Lorne.

international journalists his impressions of the Canadian Northwest. Stamp calls it "the most inspired speech of his life." It was published by the department of agriculture in Ottawa, and by 1883 it had had three printings.

On his return to Ottawa, Lorne warned the government that a clash was impending between settlers and

Native peoples. His advice was ignored with disastrous results. Four years later the Northwest Rebellion erupted. In November, the governor general took eight weeks' leave. Reunited with the princess in England, he saw for himself her state of health. "Louise is still very weak and is good for nothing, but is slowly mending," he wrote.

Her Royal Highness was back in Canada by June 5, 1882. Rumours of a Fenian plot against her kept

Arch of Welcome to Princess Louise and the Marquis of Lorne at Cary Castle, British Columbia's government house in Victoria, 1882.

the princess at the Citadel. August 30, she and Lorne set out for a major tour of British Columbia. The railway was still unfinished so they travelled through the United States, which gave them a chance to see California. From San Francisco, HMS *Comus* took them by sea to Victoria, September 20, where they made a joyful entry into the city. Louise was Victoria's first princess.

On September 28, Her Royal Highness accompanied the governor general to New Westminster, named by her mother over two decades earlier. Accepting gifts from the wife of the Seebeldts chief, Louise shook hands with her. The woman was overcome by a courtesy she never experienced from local whites. When Lorne set out on a solo tour of the British Columbia interior, which took him up the Fraser and Thompson Rivers to Shuswap and Okanagan lakes, the princess remained in Victoria. Its near perfect climate nourished her health and she was able to lead a busy but relatively informal life, painting, sketching, and turning up unannounced at public events. Cary Castle, the province's government house, she described as "halfway between heaven and Balmoral."

View from Government House, Victoria. A watercolour by Her Royal Highness Princess Louise.

Princess Louise with a party at the Rideau Hall toboggan slide.

Lord Lorne declared the Royal Canadian Academy of Arts open.

She and Lorne happily prolonged their residence in the province until December 7. The governor general saw the urgency of countering growing British Columbia secessionism over the Canadian government's failure to keep its promise to complete the transcontinental railway by 1881. It was a real threat. Beaver, the provincial premier, is said to have suggested his province leave Confederation and set up an independent kingdom with Louise as queen. Lorne convinced Ottawa of the need to push ahead with the line. His advice was heeded. It was one of his major successes. After a private holiday in California, Princess Louise wintered in Bermuda and Lorne went back to Ottawa.

Louise rejoined him at Rideau Hall in April, just in time to entertain her lively nephew, Prince George of Wales. They made a summer residence in Quebec and fished on the Cascapedia. Lorne unexpectedly declined to accept an additional sixth year as governor general. Elizabeth Longford has pointed out that Princess Louise's annoyance with her husband for not consulting her about this decision gives the lie to allegations

that she disliked Canada. She was disappointed and did mind leaving — a lot. Queen Victoria's opinion was that Lorne was jealous of Louise's success with Canadians, for when present she invariably eclipsed him.

On arriving in Canada, Princess Louise and her husband were determined to create a national association of Canadian artists so that "we shall have a school here worthy of our beloved dominion." The Royal

Canadian Academy, nucleus of the National Gallery of Canada, was the result. It held its first exhibition in Ottawa, March 6, 1880, and Lorne asked Queen Victoria to bestow the designation Royal on it. Though unable to attend the opening because of her accident, Louise, in Lorne's words, "insisted that I should bring up to her room nearly every one of the pictures exhibited, in order that she might judge the position of Canadian art at the time." She gave many of her own works to the exhibitions and to art galleries in the country.

Lorne's second achievement was the Royal Society of Canada, inaugurated in the senate chamber, May 25, 1882. The Royal Society, which brought together scholars and scientists, planted the seeds of National Museums of Canada, the National Library of Canada, and Public Archives Canada. It was a formidable achievement.

A round of farewell visits to Toronto and Montreal, and a call for the beautification of the capital, wound up the Lornes's time in office. In his farewell address to the senate and commons, the governor general described their period in Canada as "the happiest five years I have ever known." Princess Louise and the marquis left Quebec City October 27, 1883, escorted to their ship through crowded streets by the Queen's Own Canadian Hussars.

Unfortunately, the years in Canada produced an estrangement between the couple. Why is not known. Princess Louise's accident was the watershed. She may just have fallen out of love with her husband. Jehanne Wake, a biographer of Louise, shows no evidence exists that the supposed discovery by the princess of Lorne's alleged — by Robert Stamp and Sandra Gwyn — homosexuality caused the break up. The real reason may have involved Louise's disappointment over her childlessness. "It was sons she sought, not lovers," Wake concludes in assessing Louise's many male friendships. Never officially separated, Lorne and Louise lived independent lives. In their later years, they came closer again, when Lorne, afflicted by Alzheimer's disease, needed his wife's care.

All eleven royalties treated in *Royal Tours 1786–2010* found that Canada gets in the blood. Lorne's promotion of Canada through his books flowered after

The princess dressed for the Canadian winter.

Marquis of Lorne talking to reporters at Rideau Hall. As governor general, he mounted a strong public relations campaign that made Canada widely known. After the publicity generated by his tour of the great north west, settlers began to flock there.

he left office. *His Memories of Canada and Scotland* was published in 1884, *Canadian Pictures Drawn with Pen and Pencil* appeared in 1894, and *Yesterday and Today in Canada* in 1910. The image he created of Canada and Canadian life remained the popular one for decades.

Princess Louise kept up with the country for the rest of her life. When Her Royal Highness died in her ninety-second year in 1939, she was colonel-in-chief of five Canadian regiments.

Chapter Five

HELPING CANADA MATURE

1883–1918

(King George V)

THE STATUTE OF WESTMINSTER of December 11, 1931, was a landmark in the development of the Commonwealth of Nations. Each of the then dominions within the British Empire and Commonwealth was recognized as equal in stature to the United Kingdom by its provisions, under the shared sovereignty of King George V. Each dominion was granted full authority over its international affairs, in addition to its domestic affairs, as had previously been the case. The king was recognized in international law as the separate embodiment of each state; for example, in the Canadian case he became the Canadian State in the eyes of the world, sixteen years before Canadian citizenship was created.

King George V was born on June 3, 1865, the second son of the Prince of Wales and grandson of Queen Victoria. He was third in line to the throne, but with an elder brother there was no expectation of his becoming king, and he was destined for a career in the Royal Navy. The death of his brother, Albert Victor, of pneumonia in 1892 changed everything. Prince George became Duke of York in 1892; and Duke of Cornwall and York and heir to the throne on January 23, 1901, following the death of

Queen Victoria and the accession of his father as King Edward VII. On November 9, 1901, he was created Prince of Wales and on May 6, 1910, he became King George V. He died on January 20, 1936, at the age of seventy.

When he was born Confederation in Canada was still two years away. When he died he was king of a fully independent Canada. He played a significant part in that profound evolution in a relatively short time and his sojourns to Canada reflected and encouraged the development.

As Prince George he first came to Canada in 1883. His aunt, Princess Louise, was chatelaine at Government House as her husband, the Marquis of Lorne, was the governor general. This first trip was an unofficial family affair. But it introduced Prince George and Canada to each other and the public was aware of his presence.

As a serving officer in the Royal Navy duty occasionally brought him to Canadian shores over the next two decades, as it had his great-granduncle a century earlier. He used the opportunity for further private visits to Canadian sites, including the city of Quebec. But the first of his two great public tours to Canada took place in the first year of the new century.

Communications Nova Scotia

Portrait of His Majesty King George V in the red chamber,
Province House, Halifax.

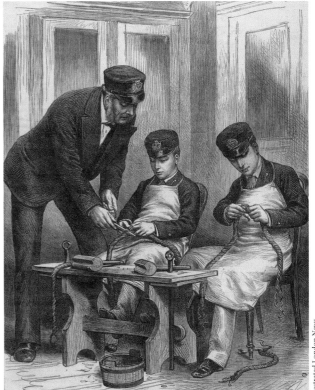

Illustrated London News

In 1878, a young Prince George and his elder brother Prince
Albert Victor literally learned the ropes in the Royal Navy.

When Queen Victoria died on January 23, 1901,
the Duke of York, then the immediate heir to the
throne, automatically assumed the title of Duke of
Cornwall. George, as Duke of Cornwall and York,
accompanied by his wife, Princess May, the Duchess
of Cornwall and York, was given the task of inaugurating the Commonwealth of Australia by opening
the first Australian parliament. The duke and duchess undertook an eight-month tour of the empire,
which the Canadian government had asked to have
Canada included in.

The RMS *Ophir*, the royal couple's seagoing home
for two thirds of that year, left Portsmouth on March
16, 1901. Exactly six months later, on September 16,
the Canadian portion of the tour began when the
Ophir dropped anchor at Quebec City. At first the
governments in London and Ottawa considered having the Canadian tour begin in the west and proceed

Archives Canada

Prince George's first trip to Canada was in 1883 to visit
his aunt, Princess Louise, and her husband, the Marquis
of Lorne, who was the governor general of Canada, at their
home at Rideau Hall in Ottawa.

The Duke and Duchess of York, Prince George and Princess May, shortly after their marriage in 1893.

eastward across the continent, as the prince's uncle, Prince Arthur, had done on a private tour in 1890. However, when South Africa was added to the worldwide tour, between the Australian and Canadian portions, it was deemed easier to begin in the east and cross the continent twice rather than sailing the *Ophir* around Cape Horn to British Columbia and then back again to Halifax to pick up the royal travellers. It was therefore decided that they would arrive in Quebec and depart from Halifax.

The weather had been horrendous as the *Ophir* approached Canada but the day of the arrival there was bright sunshine. The *Ophir* was escorted by a cruiser and four destroyers. An additional five destroyers (one French) were present in Quebec's harbour to welcome the ship. The tour organizer, Joseph Pope (later Sir Joseph), the Canadian undersecretary of state (equivalent today to the deputy minister of Canadian heritage) wrote that, "Never before in the recollection of living men had so many British men-of-war assembled at one time in the port of Quebec."

HMS Ophir, *the floating home for the Duke and Duchess of Cornwall and York on their 1901 worldwide tour, left England from Portsmouth harbour.*

The tour began under a pall of sadness, however. As the royal party approached Quebec, word was conveyed to them that the American president, William McKinley, had been assassinated. The duke and duchess were greeted on board by the governor general, Lord Minto, and the prime minster, Sir Wilfrid Laurier. In accordance with the king's wishes, the heir to the throne was to take precedence over the governor general while he was in Canada.

When the duke departed the ship he was wearing the uniform of an Admiral of the Fleet, the duchess was dressed simply in black. The period of court mourning for Queen Victoria's death had not yet expired, which dictated the dress. Also, throughout the tour there were to be no balls or public banquets, as originally planned, only official dinners, concerts, receptions, and reviews. The royal party included the duchess's

THE OPHIR IN DOCK AT HALIFAX

HMS Ophir at dock in Halifax for an overhaul while the duke and duchess were touring Canada, a drawing by Petty Officer Harry Price of the Ophir, who kept an account of the 1901 tour.

brother, Prince Alexander of Teck, who would himself return to Canada in 1940 as governor general, when he was known as the Earl of Athlone.

In his response to the welcome the prince spoke both of his past visits and the shocking news from south of the border:

> … We wish to acknowledge with gratitude the hearty welcome accorded to us by the vast crowds which today throng your beautifully decorated streets.… It is a great pleasure to find myself here again for a third time, and that on this occasion the duchess is with me; and that we together will enjoy the memorable associations and natural beauties of this ancient city and its picturesque surroundings.… I take this, the first opportunity, to express, in common with the whole civilized world, my horror at the detestable crime which has plunged into mourning the great friendly nation on your border, and has robbed the United States of the precious life of their first magistrate …

Speaking of the contributions of Canadians in the South African War that was still underway, the prince also alluded in a martial vein to the defence of Canada in the American Revolution and the War of 1812, when the United States was not a "friendly nation":

> The blood shed on the battlefields in South Africa may, like that shed by your fathers in 1775 and 1812, weave fresh strands in the cord of brotherhood that binds together our glorious empire.

There was a review of over 4,000 troops and sailors on the Plains of Abraham at which the prince invested Lieutenant R.E.W. Turner with the Victoria Cross for his bravery at Lillefontein in South Africa.

In a speech at Laval University the prince took the opportunity to praise the role of the Catholic Church in Canadian life:

71

At the Canadian capital city the duke and duchess ran the timber slides on the Ottawa River.

Archives Canada

I am glad to acknowledge the noble part which the Catholic Church in Canada has played throughout its history. The hallowed memories of its martyred missionaries are a priceless heritage, and in the great and beneficent work of education and in implanting and fostering a spirit of patriotism and loyalty, it has rendered signal service to Canada and the Empire.

Abundant proof of the success of your efforts has been afforded by the readiness with which the French Canadians have sprung to arms and shed their blood, not only in times long gone by, but also in the present day on behalf of their king and his empire.

If the crown has faithfully and honourably fulfilled its engagement to protect and respect your faith, the Catholic church has amply fulfilled its obligation not only to teach reverence for law and order, but to instil a sentiment of loyalty and devotion into the minds of those to whom it ministers.

A decade later, as King George V, the prince would give substance to his respect for the Catholic Church when he forced the parliament at Westminster to drop the anti-Catholic portion of the parliamentary oath required of monarchs by refusing to meet parliament until they did so.

The royal couple arrived in Quebec on September 16 and travelled west on a specially built royal train. It consisted of ten cars and was 250 metres long. The duke and duchess's private day coach was called the "Cornwall" and their night coach the "York." Recalling the overall tour and the empire, other cars were named "Canada," "Australia," "South Africa," "India," and "Sandringham." There was mahogany and walnut panelling throughout and electric lighting. The *Winnipeg Tribune*, with great enthusiasm, said that it was "the most magnificent product of railroad architecture ever seen on the continent, which is the equivalent to saying the whole world."

The praise of the train was not simply journalistic exaggeration. The tour was carried on the Canadian Pacific Railway and the CPR was important for both

Canada and the empire. Successive Canadian governments, back to the days of Sir John A. Macdonald, had argued that building the CPR was Canada's contribution to imperial security when London asked for greater military expenditures. The tour served as an opportunity for the company, the Canadian government, and the Canadian people to show it off.

In Ottawa, during a visit to the parliament buildings, the prince used the opportunity to praise the creation, expansion, and aspirations of Canada that had taken place in his own lifetime:

> It is especially gratifying to me to meet you here on the threshold of the building, the corner stone of which was laid by my dear father. Standing here in the capital of Canada, in the shadow of this noble pile, it is impossible without a feeling of pride to reflect how far short of the actual results were the hopes and aspirations of that day, now more than forty years ago. Ottawa was then but the capital of two provinces yoked together in an uneasy union. Today it is the capital of a great and prosperous dominion stretching from the Atlantic to the Pacific ocean; the centre of the political life and administration of a contented and united people. The federation of Canada stands preeminent among the political events of the century just closed, for its fruitful and beneficent results on the life of the people concerned. As in ancient times, by the union of Norman and Saxon, the English nation was produced, so by the federation of Canada the two great nations which form its population have been welded into a harmonious people, and afforded free play and opportunity to contribute each its best service to the public well-being. Creditable as this achievement is to the practical wisdom and patriotism of the statesmen who founded the union and who have since guided its destinies, it is no less honourable to the people upon whose support they had to rely, and who have in a spirit of mutual toleration and sympathy, sustained them in the great work of union. This spirit is no less necessary than it was in the past, and I am confident that the two races will continue, each according to its special genius and opportunity, to aid and co-operate in building up the great edifice of which the foundations have been so well and truly laid.

Wheat arch in the city of Winnipeg erected for the royal tour of 1901.

73

The theme of Canada's achievements and progress within the memory of just one or two generations was a constant one on the tour, and even more so in western Canada, which was even younger than the east. In Winnipeg the prince compared the city with what he had known as a youth:

> During the long and memorable journey to the extreme eastern and from thence to the far western limit of our vast empire, we have seen everywhere many and varied proofs of its steady but certain progress, material and political, but I doubt whether in the whole course of that experience a more striking example is to be found than in the comparison of the Fort Garry of our childhood with the Winnipeg of today. Then, as you say, "A village hamlet in solitude," broken only by the presence of "the passing hunter and fur trader," today the busy centre of what has become the great granary of the empire, the political centre of an active and enterprising population in the full enjoyment of the privileges and institutions of British citizenship.

As the train brought the duke and duchess to Saskatchewan they were treated to an early Canadian snowfall; they looked out from the train on the morning of September 27 to see the prairies covered in snow. But it had melted by the time they debarked in Regina. In his speech at Government House he contrasted "the free, healthy and useful life which is enjoyed in this country with the narrow, and alas! too often, unwholesome existence of the thousands in our great cites at home."

In Vancouver's Stanley Park the prince had a picture taken of a giant hollowed-out tree with a circumference of twenty-three metres at its base, into which a horse and carriage were placed with two members of the royal suite seated in the carriage. On the return trip through Ontario, the royal couple was welcomed by a large crowd in Toronto, despite a heavy rain. The *Times* correspondent wrote, "Rain did its best to spoil yesterday's welcome, but the children singing in the

The Sphere

On September 28 the duke received Chief Bull's Head at a pow-wow near the Rocky Mountains.

Archives Canada

At York Lodge, the shooting box named in his honour at Poplar Point near Banff, Alberta, the royal duke tried his hand in a canoe en route to the shooting grounds on October 6.

vast amphitheatre round the station, and waving Union Jacks and maple branches, formed the prettiest sight I have ever seen." There was a reception in the legislative chamber at which 2,000 people passed before the throne.

The conclusion of the tour in the Maritimes included stops in Saint John, New Brunswick, and Halifax, Nova Scotia. The travel logistics regrettably precluded a visit to Prince Edward Island, but an

Archives Canada

In London, Ontario, the duke presented colours to the 7th Regiment Fusiliers (now 4th Battalion, The Royal Canadian Regiment).

address from the provincial government was presented by its lieutenant-governor in Halifax. The prince expressed his regret at not being able to see the province of which he had "pleasant associations" from an earlier private visit when he had been in Canada.

Before departing Halifax on the *Ophir* the duke wrote a letter to the governor general in which he told Lord Minto, "Before leaving Canada I am anxious to make known, through you, with what regret the duchess and I bid farewell to a people who, by their warmheartedness and cordiality, have made us feel at home amongst them from the first moment of our arrival on their shores."

The final stop before England was in St. John's, Newfoundland, where the royal couple received an unusual gift to complete their worldwide tour — a nine-month-old Newfoundland dog to take back to their seven-year-old son Prince Edward.

The Duke of Cornwall and York kept a methodical record of the activities on the tour of Canada, and the statistics give some indication of the gruelling nature of royal progresses in that era. The prince shook hands with 24,855 people at official receptions and received 544 addresses; he laid twenty-one foundation stones and gave one hundred speeches; he presented 4,329 medals and distributed 140 titles.

The 1901 tour was described by its Canadian organizer, Sir Joseph Pope, as "a stately pageant, a unique spectacle, a royal progress the like of which Caesar had never dreamed."

Toronto Daily Star *souvenir number published the itinerary of the royal visit to Toronto.*

"The prince and people have been delighted with each other and have enthused each other. The Prince of Wales has taught the people of Quebec how to cheer." That was how the governor general, Lord Grey, described the day to the king in his letter of July 31. The prince noted, "I hope my visit has done good, especially to improve the relations between the English and French Canadians, which have never been so good as they are now."

As part of the celebrations the prince presented a cheque for 90,000 pounds, which was donated by people from around the empire to assist the Canadian government in its purchase of the lands to establish the Quebec battlefields park. In a concrete way the gift showed the kinship that the people of the empire

In 1860, when the government of the province of Canada had asked Queen Victoria to come to the North American territory, she had responded by sending her son the Prince of Wales in her stead. Forty-eight years later, the government of the dominion of Canada asked King Edward VII, that former Prince of Wales, to preside at the tercentenary celebrations of the city of Quebec. History repeated itself and the king sent his son, the new Prince of Wales, in his own stead. Prince George, the Duke of Cornwall and York on his last trip to Canada in 1901, had been created Prince of Wales by the king in November 1901, shortly after the conclusion of that trip.

It was a short but significant trip to Canada in July 1908, limited just to the ceremony in Quebec City. The Prince of Wales arrived in the new fast cruiser HMS *Indomitable*. The review of the Canadian militia on the Plains was a spectacular demonstration of Canada's martial spirit in the first decade of the new century.

King Louis XIV Canadian Royal Heritage Archives

The Prince of Wales, after being granted the title by the king.

Above: *Painting by J.D. Kelly and A.H. Hider of the Prince of Wales on horseback at the 1908 review of the Canadian militia on the Plains of Abraham, an occasion of grand pageantry for the tercentenary celebrations of the City of Quebec.*

Right: *Accompanied by General (later Sir) Arthur Currie (centre, walking on the wooden planks) and General Horne, King George V (left, walking in the mud) inspected the battlefield of Vimy, where his Canadian troops under General Sir Julian Byng (later Baron Byng of Vimy) and his deputy General Currie had achieved a great victory in the First World War.*

Royal Archives

felt towards each other in the first decade of the twentieth century.

The 1908 celebration turned out to be George's last trip to Canada. Two years later he was the king. Canadians came to London in large number, in the official delegation and privately, for his coronation in 1911, and the king and queen then went to India for the Delhi Durbar to celebrate his status as Emperor of India. A trip to Canada would undoubtedly have occurred in due course but the First World War descended on the world in 1914 and put all normal activities on hold for four years.

But in a sense the king did visit Canada. For those four years the youth of Canada were not in their homes but fighting in the mud of France and

Left: *On another visit to the Western Front during the First World War, the king inspected captured German trenches.*

Below: *Paintings of King George V and Queen Mary adorn the walls in the Senate foyer of the parliament buildings in Ottawa.*

Flanders. King George V made several tours of the Western Front where he met soldiers from Canada and the other dominions and colonies. On one of those tours he was thrown from his horse and seriously injured. He was tended to in a field hospital by a Canadian nurse, Viviane Tremaine. Although he recovered, he suffered back problems for the rest of his life and the injury precluded a return to North America in the postwar years.

Although he did not tour Canada again, the king ensured that his sons did and he supported a major addition to the symbolic imagery of Canada. In 1921 he assumed royal arms as the King of Canada, anticipating the developments that would culminate in the Statute of Westminster a decade later. These replaced the use of a shield that merely combined the provincial arms. Surmounted by the royal crown, incorporating elements of the ancient arms of Britain and France as well as distinctive Canadian elements, the royal arms were a visual interpretation of the new status of Canada demonstrated in and enhanced by his pre-war royal tours and then firmly entrenched by the achievements of Canadian soldiers in the war. The king also adopted white and red as his official royal colours for Canada to honour Canadian sacrifice in the Great War. These colours would be the basis of the national flag of Canada adopted more than half a century later.

Chapter Six

"CANADIAN" GOVERNOR

1869–1916

(Prince Arthur, Duke of Connaught)

THE TENTH GOVERNOR GENERAL of Canada from Confederation was His Royal Highness Prince Arthur, Duke of Connaught and Strathearn. He was the third son of Queen Victoria and was born on May 1, 1850, the eighty-first birthday of the first Duke of Wellington, the hero of the Battle of Waterloo. The Iron Duke, as Wellington was known, was the royal baby's godfather and the prince was named Arthur in honour of his connection with the empire's greatest soldier.

By design or coincidence this association with Wellington presaged Prince Arthur's future. He was to be a soldier and intimately connected with Canada. Wellington's reputation as a soldier is well-known. Less well-known is the important role he played in the development of Canada in the early and mid-nineteenth century. In 1819 he developed the defence plan for Canada that resulted in the fortresses of Quebec, Kingston, and Halifax. As head of the Ordnance Department he was responsible for the building of the Rideau Canal in Upper Canada (now Ontario) and as British prime minister he governed the whole empire, including the British North American provinces, in the great matters of state.

Prince Arthur entered the Royal Military College at Woolwich in 1868, became a lieutenant in the Royal Engineers, and then a captain in the Rifle Brigade. He became a lieutenant-colonel in 1876, a general in 1893, and a field marshal in 1904. Along the way were colonial battles such at Tel-el-Kebir and postings such as commander-in-chief in Ireland, inspector general of the Imperial Forces, and commander-in-chief of the Mediterranean area.

As it had been for his grandfather, the army was responsible for Prince Arthur's first arrival in Canada. He came as an officer assigned to the Montreal detachment of the Rifle Brigade. There was some concern over the possibility that Fenian sympathizers in the United States might attempt to do the prince harm but those concerns were overruled by the decision that his military duty was more important.

After an eight day sail Prince Arthur arrived in Halifax. For the next eight weeks he took the role of a royal prince and toured the country, visiting Prince Edward Island, Pictou, Shediac, Saint John, Fredericton, Woodstock, Grand Falls, Quebec, Petrolia, London, Niagara Falls, Buffalo (New York), Paris, Brantford,

Silk cigarette souvenir from the First World War of H.R.H. the Duke of Connaught as governor general. In the background is the Canadian Red Ensign of 1867–1924.

Arthur, 1st Duke of Wellington, presents a gift to his namesake, Prince Arthur, held by Queen Victoria, at the royal child's baptism.

Prince Arthur depicted in winter dress in Canada as an officer of the Rifle Brigade in March 1870.

Hamilton, Toronto, and Ottawa and then joining his regiment in Montreal. He also visited New York and Washington, D.C., where he and the president, Ulysses S. Grant, met in January 1870. Returning to Montreal on February 7, he went on to Ottawa a few days later to attend the opening of parliament, the first member of the royal family to do so in Canada.

Of Montreal the prince wrote, "Most anxious am I to consider for the time being Montreal as my home, and to lose no opportunity of becoming full acquainted with its institutions, its people, and its commerce. The selection of Montreal as my residence is sufficient proof of the confidence Her Majesty places in the devotion of the city to her throne."

When the Fenians attacked Canada in 1870 Prince Arthur took part with his regiment in the battle of Eccles Hill, May 25, near Montreal. Historians have disputed how active a role he took but this may have been caused by a letter he wrote to his mother in which he downplayed his involvement, saying that he had

Above: *Prince Arthur turned the first sod at the opening of the Toronto, Grey and Bruce Railway, Weston, Ontario, October 5, 1869.*

Right: *The Duke of Connaught joined fellow veterans of the Fenian Raids at a 1911 ceremony in Queen's Park, Toronto, in front of the statue of his mother Queen Victoria.*

taken no part in the actual fighting himself. However, this was perhaps the case of a son not wishing to worry his mother. Other accounts record his active participation and on another occasion Arthur wrote that he had difficulty preventing his troops from firing while the Fenians were still on the American side of the border but that once they crossed, "We opened fire and they rapidly broke up." In any event, he received the Fenian Medal awarded to those who took part in the battle and the experience instilled in him a belief in the future of Canada and made him an advocate for Canadian unity and development both in Britain and when he later returned to Canada.

On his appointment as governor general in 1911, Pauline Johnson, the Mohawk poetess of Canada, whose work helped reconcile the cultural differences between aboriginal and settler Canadians told of another honour received by the Prince in 1869.

Arthur, Duke of Connaught, is the only living white man who today has an undisputed right to the title of "Chief of the Six Nations Indians" (known collectively as the Iroquois). He possesses the privilege of sitting in their councils, of casting his vote on all matters relative to the governing of the tribes … In short, were every drop of blood in his royal veins red, instead of blue, he could not be more fully qualified as an Indian chief than he now is, not even were his title one of the fifty hereditary ones whose illustrious names composed the Iroquois confederacy before the paleface ever set foot in America.

It was on the occasion of his first visit to Canada in 1869, when he was little more than a boy, that [the Iroquois on the Grand River Reserve] had a request to make of him; would he accept the title of chief and visit their reserve to give them the opportunity of conferring? … It was on the morning of October 1 … that a chief of each of the three "clans" of the Mohawks [the chief of the Bear clan, the chief of the Turtle clan, and Onwanonsyshon, father of Pauline Johnson, the chief of the Wolf clan] … received the prince into the Mohawk tribe, conferring upon him the name of "Kavakoudge" which means "the sun flying from east to west under the guidance of the Great Spirit." The constitution that Hiawatha had founded centuries ago, a constitution wherein fifty chiefs, no more, no less, should form the parliament of the Six Nations had been shattered and broken, because this race of loyal red men desired to do honour to a slender young boy-prince, who now bears the fifty-first title of the Iroquois.

Many white men have received from these same people honorary titles, but none

has been bestowed through the ancient ritual, with the imperative members of the three clans assisting, save that borne by Arthur of Connaught.

The prince himself recalled his youthful time in Canada half a century later, on September 5, 1916, at his farewell visit to the Canadian National Exhibition, when his tenure as governor general was coming to an end:

It is with the greatest regret of both the duchess and my daughter and myself that we are leaving the Canadian shore … I have the Canadian Fenian Medal for services in 1869/70 and I spent a year with my regiment in Montreal. My first visit to Toronto was when I accompanied the then governor general, Lord Lisgar, who paid his first visit to Toronto as governor general, and I was with him in the carriage. I can well remember the splendid reception we received. I merely mention this as I should not like you to think that I am a relatively new Canadian. In coming back I came to a country which I knew fairly well and which had already shown to me the greatest kindness. The duchess came through here in the year '90 when we had a pleasant stay in Toronto, I think it was in June and it was beautiful weather, and I remember very well the procession of troops and firemen.

The 1890 tour he referred to was a cross-country excursion from west to east when the prince and his wife, Princess Louise of Prussia, whom he had married in 1879, had the opportunity to see much of the country. It produced an immediate and enduring love for the Canadian west in both of them, which they were able to enhance when they returned to Canada as viceroy and chatelaine. They were returning to England from an army posting in India and they were entranced by the Rocky Mountains and Niagara Falls, and were feted in Toronto, Ottawa, and Montreal. They left from Quebec after "a marvellous trip."

Royal Archives

Left: *Prince Arthur, Duke of Connaught's arrival at Quebec City in 1911. He is led down the gangplank by his aide-de-camp Lieutenant Commander Alexander Ramsay, who would become his son-in-law in 1919.*

Below: *The Duke of Connaught was installed as the governor general at a ceremony in the legislative council chamber in Quebec on October 11, 1911, with the duchess beside him.*

Archives Canada

The duke, the duchess, and Princess Patricia, their twenty-five-year-old youngest daughter, arrived at Quebec on October 13, 1911, and the duke was sworn into office in the Parliament of Quebec. Through a failure in the organization of the arrival the carriage that was to meet them was fifteen minutes late arriving but they good-naturedly waited. Only a few weeks after establishing himself in Ottawa the duke presided over the opening of parliament in a grand ceremony, reflecting the pageantry of the king's coronation earlier in the year. The duke wore his uniform as a field marshal. The duchess wore the dress that she had worn at the coronation, a practice that was repeated with even more significance in 1957 when Queen Elizabeth II opened the Canadian parliament for the first time and wore her coronation dress.

Remembering his enjoyment of the 1890 trip the duke had considered making a trip to the west right away. Lord Grey, his predecessor as governor general, recommended against it. Lord Grey feared that eastern Canada would be upset, as the older part of the dominion, if it did not receive the first tour. He used an interesting analogy with the prince, comparing eastern Canada to an old established matron at a party who would be upset, "If she were to see Your Royal Highness pass her by, and take in to dinner the youngest beauty of the party."

So the first tour in 1911 was limited to Toronto, Hamilton, and Kingston, followed by Montreal on November 27. In May 1912 the duke undertook a tour to Winnipeg followed by the Maritimes. The duchess was to accompany him but she suddenly took ill and the doctors were not sure why, so her place was taken by Princess Patricia. Then, on August 28, the royal family, the duchess now feeling well again, headed west. Included in the tour were Sault Ste. Marie, Prince Arthur (named after the duke), Saskatoon, Prince Albert, Edmonton, Calgary, Banff, Vancouver, a cruise to Prince Rupert, Victoria (including an inspection of the fledgling Royal Canadian Navy in Esquimalt), and, on the return trip, Medicine Hat, Regina, and Brandon. After a return to Toronto,

The Duke of Connaught (front row centre), the Duchess of Connaught (to his left), and Princess Patricia (to his right) posed in the Canadian countryside with their staff in the winter of 1912–13.

On their 1916 trip to Banff, Alberta, the duke and duchess watched Indian races from the back seat of their automobile.

they headed back to Ottawa and were home again at Rideau Hall in November. On the tour the duke gave several hundred speeches. The duke and duchess returned to the west in August 1914 and again in May 1916 for holidays in Banff. In 1914 the duke also visited both Newfoundland and Labrador, although they were not then part of Canada

In January 1912 he had also accepted a private invitation from a friend in New York, but what was officially a private visit became a public relations success as additional invitations flowed in from Americans when his plans were made known and thousands turned out in New York to see him. He also accepted an invitation to Washington, D.C., to see the American president, W.H. Taft.

Rideau Hall was at best a modest residence for a member of the royal family as it was for all its less exalted occupants and it was even more modest in the early twentieth century than it is in the early twenty-first.

The first impression one gets of Government House … is not a very grand one, in fact one wonders if one has made a mistake and come

Princess Patricia, an accomplished artist, had a studio at Rideau Hall. Here she is shown painting an Ottawa scene from the veranda roof of the long gallery at the residence.

86

up to a gymnasium flanked by a riding school with a very poor little porch connecting the two!! It is painted a slate grey and the porch a dirty brown of no particular shade!! So this is our house in Canada. Inside the entrance is not imposing either — but then one goes into the drawing room, the smaller one called the blue room, my sitting room and A[rthur]'s study which are all good sized and comfortable — the day was so sunny that it gave us a bright and cheerful impression and I feel we shall be very happy here.

That was the first impression of the duchess. It was during the Connaught era that the Rideau Hall Canadians know today was created, as a grand new façade, referencing the façade of Buckingham Palace created at the same time, was added. Planned under Lord Grey, it addressed much of the problem cited by the duchess in her observation.

In Canada the duke took up skating and added skating parties to the social calendar at Rideau Hall. They were a Canadian version of European court balls, the grounds decorated with Chinese lanterns and three huge bonfires burning. A supper in the curling hut complemented the festivities. Up to a thousand people attended these spectacularly popular events. The duke maintained a regular routine of four days a week at his parliamentary office and invited senators and members of parliament of both parties in small groups to private receptions.

The duke, the duchess, and Princess Patricia took to Canadian life, including camping in the forests, fishing, and canoeing. One anecdote about the duke's fishing experiences endeared him to Canadians. In 1914 he was having a most successful day at Consolation Lake, near Banff and Lake Louise. The governor general had exceeded the legal per-day quota and was approached by the park warden who suggested he should therefore stop fishing.

"Per angler, per day, perdition; my good man, I ask you what is the sense of me being governor of this widespread, far-flung, sea-to-sea dominion if I cannot catch all the fish I have a mind to?" the duke replied in mock indignation. But, of course, he stopped fishing.

Princess Patricia was a great asset to the Duke of Connaught during his tenure at Rideau Hall. Young, pretty, and vivacious, she threw herself fully into the life of Ottawa and the country as a whole and captured the hearts of Canadians. Her love of sports and the outdoors made her at one with the society she was living in. She was also an accomplished artist. During the First World

Princess Patricia, daughter of the Duke of Connaught, on the 1917 Canadian dollar bill.

War she worked for the Canadian Red Cross and after her return to England in 1916 she worked at the Maple Leaf Club for Canadian soldiers in London and the Canadian Hospital in Orpington, among other activities helping Canadian soldiers. In Canada she also fell in love with Lieutenant Commander (later Admiral) the Hon. Alexander Ramsay, a Royal Navy aide to her father. He was the third son of the thirteenth Earl of Dalhousie and the great-grandnephew of George Ramsay, ninth Earl of Dalhousie and governor-in-chief of Canada, 1819–28. In 1919 she gave up her official royal style and they married. She subsequently took the title Lady Patricia Ramsay and remained an active member of the extended royal family until her death.

The duchess's health never fully improved from the 1912 scare and in January 1913 she was hospitalized. In March 1913 the Connaughts returned to London for her health and she underwent surgery. The duke was torn between trying "to do what is right, both as regards my duty as governor general and also as a husband." He wished to complete his agreed two years period as governor but offered to resign. The Canadian government, not wanting to cut their tenure short, encouraged them to take as much time in England as they needed for the duchess to recuperate. Throughout this period the governor general and the prime minister, Sir Robert Borden, kept in regular contact on government affairs by cable. The duchess's recovery was slow and she suffered a relapse requiring a second operation, which extended the stay until the fall. By that time the October wedding of their son Prince Arthur to his cousin Princess Alexandra, Duchess of Fife, a granddaughter of King Edward VII, had taken place. Finally the duchess's condition improved remarkably and they returned to Canada in late October. By then the Duke of Connaught had also agreed to a one-year extension of their tenure at Rideau Hall to October 1914.

It has sometimes been suggested by critics of the Duke of Connaught that he did not understand the limitations of his office and upset ministers by trying to interfere in government affairs and, during the war, believed his role as commander-in-chief was substantive and not honorary. However, there is little evidence

The coat of arms of the Duke of Connaught is carved in stone on the Duke of Connaught School in the east end of Toronto.

to support this. The governor, like the king, had the right to be consulted, to encourage and to warn, and the duke never went beyond that.

Most of his trouble was with the minister of Militia, Sir Sam Hughes. Known in his own time as "Mad Sam Hughes," few students of the period would doubt today that he was at least mentally erratic if not certifiably insane. The duke simply recognized the situation earlier than most and warned the prime minister when Hughes's erratic behaviour caused dangerous policies. He believed it was his duty to do so. But Hughes was a powerful politician at the time and his supporters criticized the duke.

Occasionally Sir Robert Borden was upset with the governor general, but that could be said of every prime minister and governor general from Confederation to today. If Sir Robert actually felt the Duke of Connaught was acting improperly he had three occasions to replace him without controversy: when the duchess's health forced the royal couple to return to England temporarily in 1913, later that year when the original two year time the duke had accepted for his appointment expired, and in August 1914 when the extension itself expired. On each occasion Sir Robert, supported

by the Canadian people, asked the Duke of Connaught to stay in Canada. The original two-year appointment became five. That would not have happened if the government thought the governor general was acting improperly or was not popular.

The duke helped raise troops during the war and strengthened their morale. Princess Patricia's Canadian Light Infantry, for example, was raised in 1914.

As a representative of the imperial government as well as of the king (the constitutional position of the governor general at the time) the duke was obliged to convey the views of London to Ottawa, but he generally took the side of Ottawa in disputes and when he disagreed with a Canadian government policy it was because he thought it bad for Canada's interests not because it offended London.

Left: *A signed photograph of the Duke of Connaught, wearing the uniform of a field marshal, was taken the year the First World War started.*

Below: *In 1915 at Rockcliffe, Ontario, the governor general and commander-in-chief inspected military equipment.*

During his time in office the boundaries of Manitoba, Ontario, and Quebec were extended and the First World War was fought. In February 1916 the centre block of the parliament buildings and the Victoria Tower were destroyed in a fire. On September 1, 1916, the governor general laid the memorial stone for the new centre block and re-laid the cornerstone placed originally by his brother King Edward VII in 1860 as Prince of Wales. The Connaught block of government buildings in the capital was named in his honour. On October 16, 1916 the duke's tenure as governor general came to an end and the Connaughts sailed for Britain.

The duchess never recovered fully from her illnesses and died five months after returning to England. The duke lived to the age of ninety-one and died on January 16, 1942. Since his son, Prince Arthur, had predeceased him in 1938, Arthur was succeeded as Duke of Connaught by his grandson Alistair, who died on April 26, 1943, at the age of twenty-eight, while serving on the Government House staff of the Earl of Athlone. Princess Patricia remained colonel-in-chief of Princess Patricia's Canadian Light Infantry until her death in 1974, when she was succeeded by her goddaughter and namesake, Patricia, Countess Mountbatten.

Prince Arthur, Duke of Connaught, the first governor general to call himself a Canadian and, as the first governor belonging to Canada's royal line, entitled to do so by status as well as sentiment, was praised by Canadians for his gracious personality, his kindness, and his interest in Canada. At a farewell dinner in 1916 in Toronto, Sir John Willison, the dinner chairman, said in his toast, "In his high office of governor general His Royal Highness has composed himself with the dignity of a prince, the sympathy of a democrat, and the courtesy of an English gentleman."

Rideau Hall, depicted before and after the grand new façade was added in 1913, was the home of the Duke and Duchess of Connaught and their daughter Princess Patricia from 1911 to 1916.

Chapter Seven

THE ONLY PROPERTY HE OWNED

1919–1962

(King Edward VIII)

FOR TWO PERIODS DURING the First World War, the heir to the throne, His Royal Highness Prince Edward, Prince of Wales, eldest son of King George V, was attached to the Canadian Corps Headquarters in Flanders. As a staff officer, he came to know Canadian troops by the thousand.

He liked them for their good nature, frankness, and fighting qualities. He and they, he felt, had a special rapport. As for the soldiers, it lifted their morale to have their king's son fight alongside them. At home, parents, wives, and sweethearts saw the young prince as a representative figure of the generation being slaughtered for freedom in the trenches of Europe. He was their hope for a better future.

When peace came, Edward set out to develop his role as Prince of Wales. He enthusiastically took up the idea of doing a series of empire tours. He would visit the demobilized soldiers and strengthen the bond of monarchy. The new and potentially dangerous aspirations for independence aroused by the war could be accommodated under the aegis of the crown. Canada, the senior overseas realm, was first on his tour list.

The result was three full-scale Canadian tours, two private sojourns there with a few official engagements, an historic encounter during his brief reign as King Edward VIII, and two private visits to the country as Duke of Windsor. In creating a unique relationship with Canada, the prince resembled his great-great grandfather, Prince Edward, the Duke of Kent, even if, in the end, his experience was less fruitful.

Slightly daunted at what lay ahead, Edward boarded HMS *Renown* and sailed August 5, 1919. At his first stop at St. John's, Newfoundland — not yet part of Canada of course — he discovered self-confidence. He found he performed well in public, impressing even dour Sir Robert Borden, the Canadian prime minister.

Soon the young prince was sufficiently at ease to enjoy himself. He was a keen observer. He chuckled over one of the Newfoundland triumphal arches of welcome when he noticed it was "largely composed of drums of cod-liver oil and hung with the carcasses of dried codfish." The third Edward involved in Canada, the prince was the first of his family to reveal his own perspective on his tours in his memoirs, *A King's Story*.

First anniversary postcard showing the Prince of Wales about to be lifted from his horse at the Canadian National Exhibition, Toronto, and passed from hand to hand over the heads of the frenzied welcoming crowd to the platform on the 1919 tour.

Prince of Wales inspected Canadian Machine Gun Battalion on the Valciennes Front in the First World War.

"Careful, Sir, you're signing the pledge!" Shouted out by someone in the crowd in Halifax, the words provoked the prince's famous flash smile, caught by the camera.

His Royal Highness's arrival on the Canadian mainland unleashed a popular frenzy. With social changes brought on by war, the formality of pre-war royal tours had crumbled. Edward was quick to notice that. What Canada wanted he wrote later was "if not a vaudeville show, then a first class carnival" — with the Prince of Wales as lead figure.

After a visit to Charlottetown, the prince reached Quebec on August 21, 1919. Tens of thousands of people lined the streets to see him. As he discovered, post-war crowds were "an almost terrifying phenomenon." They repeatedly broke through and swamped police lines, snatching at Edward's handkerchief, trying to tear buttons from his coat, even scratching his neck in their attempts to touch him.

Their hysteria obscured the serious side of the tour; his bilingual speech in Montreal for instance. In it he declared that the union of French and English in Canada was not just political convenience but "an example of the highest wisdom." He hated to see his presentation of posthumous medals to mothers and fathers of soldiers who didn't return from the war go largely ignored.

King Louis XIV Canadian Royal Heritage Archives

The outrageous 1919 Toronto crowd.

Sir Joseph Pope, the elderly civil servant who organized the 1919 tour, was appalled. "I simply cannot understand what has happened to the Canadian people, Sir," he lamented. Pope insisted the prince appear at events on horseback. Edward feared the uncontrollable crowds might cause the horses to panic and trample people underfoot.

The crunch came at Toronto, August 26, when Edward inaugurated Warriors' Day at the Canadian National Exhibition. Twenty-seven thousand veterans massed for the climax of the event. When the prince appeared on horseback, the ex-servicemen broke rank and seized him. "The next thing I knew I was being lifted off the horse's back by strong hands and passed like a football over the heads of the veterans to the platform," wrote His Royal Highness. In a flash, cheering turned to laughter. The horse disappeared. So did a mortified Sir Joseph. Neither was seen again.

A change in tour arrangements took shape with Pope's replacement. The Prince of Wales proceeded west by Canadian Pacific Railway. His quarters on the train were in the last car, with an observation platform at the back. From it he could deliver impromptu three-minute speeches at the innumerable stops where crowds gathered along the route.

"Getting off the train to stretch my legs I would start up conversations with farmers, section hands, miners, small-town editors, or newly arrived immigrants from Europe" he recalled. He was taking the pulse of the country. His first days in Canada "were in some ways the most exhilarating that I have ever known." Canadians convinced him that they liked him for himself, "an act of open-heartedness that did my ego no end of good."

"Put it there, Ed. I shook hands with your grandfather." Confronted by a man from the crowd shooting out his hand early in the tour, the Prince decided it behooved him to shake hands. In a week his right hand was blackened and swollen. If he continued to use it, the doctor said, it might be permanently disabled. His Royal Highness retired the hand from service. He employed his left instead.

"I want Canada to look upon me as Canadian" was the theme of Prince of Wales's tour. If "not actually

Welcome arch at Edmonton for the prince, 1919.

Canadian born, I'm a Canadian in mind and spirit." His boyish shyness, blue eyes, and lovely complexion, his courtesy and thoughtfulness captivated everyone. A weltschmerz was detected in his eye. "Evanescent, bewildering, rippling and swirling like a mountain stream," Philip Ziegler, his official biographer, describes his extraordinary personality.

The apogee of Edward's love affair with Canada came when the royal train arrived at Calgary, September 14. There the prince became enamoured of the lifestyle of the west. The space and tranquility, the mystique, vigour, and apparent freedom captured his imagination. "That's a real life," he wrote to his mother, Queen Mary, adding, "I am now rapidly becoming a westerner." For a respite he visited the Bar-U Ranch near High River. His host, George Lane, was the founder of the Calgary Stampede.

Edward left the Bar-U for the Stony Indians in Banff, who made him Chief Morning Star. On the train to Vancouver, thinking over his experience of the ranch, he decided to ask Lane to meet him at Fort McLeod

Giving medals on the 1919 tour.

on his return. When he did, he commissioned Lane to purchase the Bedingfeld property at Pekisko near the Bar-U, a ranch set in foothills with the Rockies rising majestically in the west behind. The ranch comprised 1,440 acres. He got it for twenty-five dollars an acre.

E.P. Ranch house enlarged by the Prince of Wales.

He renamed the property the E.P. Ranch after his formal signature "Edward, P." — "P" for Prince. It would become the most famous ranch in Canada. "The atmosphere of western Canada appeals to me intensely," he told a spellbound audience in Winnipeg, announcing his purchase. "The free, vigorous, hopeful spirit of westerners not only inspires me, but makes me feel happy and at home."

The 1919 tour continued until November 10. It was punctuated by those personal touches the Prince of Wales was so good at. Scrambling to catch the cap of a soldier in a wheelchair that had been snatched

1980s Postcard showing the setting of the E.P. Ranch under the ownership of the Duke of Windsor's successors. The original ranch house is the white building on the middle left.

95

The prince at the E.P. Ranch.

off by the wind or personally taking part in bronco busting in Saskatoon.

Before heading west, the prince had performed other important acts. Though it was applauded at the time, it has been forgotten that he led the Labour Day Parade in Ottawa. The Winnipeg General Strike had occurred earlier in the year, raising the spectre of red revolution and communism in Canada. Edward's decision to lead the parade was more than an act of sympathy. It reaffirmed that at the non-partisan level of national life which the crown provided, labour was seen as belonging.

Also in Ottawa, he laid the cornerstone of the Peace Tower. The tower was to be the centerpiece in the rebuilt central block of the parliament buildings of Canada, destroyed by fire in 1916. The inscription from Psalm 72 for the structure alluded to the prince: "Give the king thy judgements, O God; and thy righteousness unto the king's son."

When it was planned, the 1919 tour made no provision for a visit to the United States. The prince pondered that omission as he was returning from British Columbia. Telegraphing the king and the governments in Ottawa and London, he obtained their approval to add eleven days for an American jaunt. This detour took him to Washington, D.C., on Armistice Day. After visiting the incapacitated Woodrow Wilson, His Royal Highness was guided about by the vice-president, Thomas Marshall.

The visit was good for Canada. Americans needed reminding of the realm on their northern border. In the United States, Edward ran up against Prohibition, which had recently been introduced. On his return to London he delighted his father with tales of life under its rigid regime. George V was tickled by a jingle Edward heard in a Canadian border town.

Four and twenty Yankees, feeling very dry,
Went across the border to get a drink of rye.
When the rye was opened, the Yanks began to
sing,
"God bless America, but God save the King!"

96

King Louis XIV Canadian Royal Heritage Archives

Top: *Laying the cornerstone of the Peace Tower, Ottawa.*

Above : *Cornerstone of the Peace Tower, Ottawa, laid by the Prince of Wales in 1919.*

Right: *Picture booklet of the 1919 tour. Sheet music for a song entitled "His Smile," profits of the sale of which went to the Soldiers' Aid Commission of Ontario.*

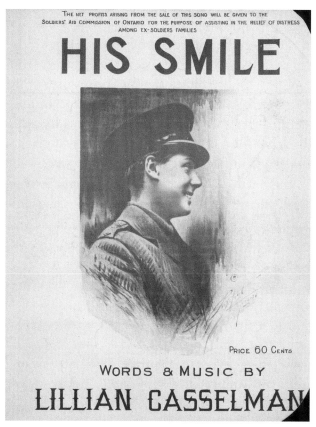

"My North American tour had taught me what was expected of a prince in the postwar world," Edward concluded. His informality of dress and manners struck the right note. Outwardly the tour was a triumph. Edward did not object to the crowds' behaviour. "In fact, I rather enjoyed it," he admitted. Mass adulation became the adrenalin to keep him going on a tour. He began to crave it.

The dose was too strong. Popular worship convinced him that his idea of updating the crown was the only right one. It fixed his thinking that he alone understood the feelings of his generation because he had suffered with them.

"You are highly strung and nervous to begin with," an adviser told him. It was true, though his passion for exercise helped alleviate it. He could not relax. The stress of tours made him depressed. He stayed up later and later, drank more whisky than was good for him. Below the surface the seemingly confident, stable young prince was an immature, "half child, half genius." Worse, he was unaware of it and seemed incapable of growing up. "I'll try to reform a bit in

Canada," he promised his mistress Freda Dudley Ward, who tried unsuccessfully to correct his more obvious faults, in 1922.

Edward suffered from a built in contradiction. In his mind he should have his own way and was stubborn about getting it. Edward's view that his right to a "life of his own" superseded royal duties was inconsistent with the vocation of a prince. The inward struggle between self-will and duty tore Edward apart. Though clever at assimilating information, he was not well-educated. Unlike his brother, Prince Albert the Duke of York, he had no religious belief to measure his actions against.

Besides being an extrovert who easily lost his temper, the Prince of Wales could be aggressive and callous. When his epileptic youngest brother, Prince John, died in 1918, Edward's insensitive letter to Queen Mary earned him her sternest reprimand. This negative side of the prince came home to his aides and advisers on the tours. They hid it and his growing discontent from the public.

It was not easy. From being bored with royal duties it was just one step to showing it and evading the responsibilities. On his 1927 Canadian tour, Edward kept everyone waiting for dinner at Government House in Ottawa until he and Prince George played a game of squash. In Montreal it was the crowds who had to wait while he golfed.

Dropping important passages from speeches painstakingly crafted by aides offended the latter and made it hard for the prince to keep first-class people in his household. Sometimes his judgement was very bad. He saw nothing risky to the monarchy in trying to arrange a meeting with Mrs. Dudley Ward in Canada during the 1919 tour.

For the next three years, Edward's life was taken up by tours to Australia, New Zealand, and India. Not until 1923 was he able to put the E.P. Ranch back on his calendar. This stay was strictly private. Travelling as "Lord Renfrew," the title used by his grandfather in 1860 in the United States, may have been a transparent incognito but it enabled the Prince of Wales to appeal to the press for a moratorium on publicity. Nothing speaks louder of Canadians' liking and respect for His Royal Highness than the fact that it was completely respected.

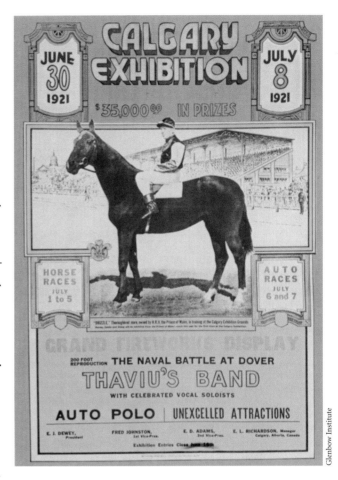

1921 Calgary Exhibition poster, featuring the Prince of Wales's thoroughbred Drizzle raised on the E.P. Ranch

Edward arrived at Quebec aboard the Canadian Pacific liner *Empress of France*, September 12, 1923, made stops in Ottawa and Winnipeg and reached Calgary on the 16th. It was harvest time at the E.P. The Prince of Wales threw himself into the work. Dressed in shabby clothes he stooked oats, chopped sunflowers, pitched hay, and filled the silo. "I've even helped muck out the cowhouse," he boasted to King George V. "I chop and saw up wood and I can assure you it is very hard work indeed!" At breakfast His Royal Highness ate flapjacks and brook trout, for lunch corn on the cob, and at dinner spuds, carrots, and beets fresh from the ground.

While eschewing official engagements, Edward gave lunches and a picnic party for rancher neighbours. "My fellow Albertans," he addressed them at the picnic, "you are welcome and I hope you enjoy your

Literary Digest

IN THE WILD AND WOOLLY
Will H. R. H. succumb to environment?

British cartoon commentary on the Prince of Wales 1923 stay at the E.P. Ranch.

Two views of the prince's lounge at the E.P. Ranch.

outing, my ranch is open to you today." He dropped in on his neighbours in his turn. The Gardner family south of the E.P. woke one morning to find the Prince of Wales eating breakfast with their ranch hands and Chinese cook, Qwon York, after an early morning ride.

His biggest entertainment was for shorthorn breeders and their families at a rodeo where the prince presented the Prince of Wales Trophy to Peter Vandermeer, overall winner of the Calgary Stampede. Reporting the event, the *Farm and Ranch Review* commented that "our shorthorn men are beginning to look to the E.P. Ranch for leadership in the contest of breeds in Alberta." So they were.

The E.P. had become important in its own right. On returning to London in 1919, the prince defended his purchase of the ranch to his skeptical father, King George V. The E.P., he explained to the king, would introduce first-class blood stock from his Cornish and Scottish estates to the Canadian ranch industry.

Strains of horses, cattle, and sheep in Alberta and the other western provinces were significantly improved because of the E.P. The influx of capital, expertise, and superior stock from the Duchy of Cornwall turned it into a centre of breeding excellence of international note. The ranch made an important ongoing contribution to agriculture too. Government, both dominion and provincial, took a fostering interest in the E.P. The rancher prince attracted maximum media attention for Canada.

There is no doubt that the ranch helped draw Edward back to Canada, though by 1924 his infatuation with it was waning. But his interest in the country was never limited to the E.P. On the Prince of Wales's 1923 stay, not only was the ranch house transformed but new flower and vegetable gardens were created

With students at the Ontario Agricultural College, Guelph.

around it with the aid of William Reader, Calgary Superintendent of Parks. The prince enjoyed the success of his ranching enterprise. He left the ranch reluctantly on September 30, returning to eastern Canada via Winnipeg, Ottawa, Montreal, and Quebec City.

His 1924 stay at the E.P. Ranch was intended to be longer than the previous one. But his Canadian journey was preceded by a visit to the United States for the international polo match. Caught up in the pulsing vitality of roaring twenties America, the pleasure-loving prince lingered on Long Island. Instead of setting out for Canada on September 7 as originally planned, it was September 29 when he crossed the border.

Tired, depressed, and suffering from a cold, the prince got to the ranch in a sleet storm. He soon revived, engaging in haymaking and walking on the hills. On his last day he opened the E.P. to the public. Five or six hundred people arrived. A stock sale was held in the afternoon. "Stop that racket!" John Durno the sale auctioneer thundered angrily when a loud argument behind his platform interrupted the proceedings. There was a muffled titter as the crowd turned to look. They found the noise was being made by the prince playing x's and o's with a group of children

In 1927 the prince made a more conventional Canadian tour. Though the hysteria of 1919 never repeated itself, there was no decline in public interest in the Prince of Wales in the later tours. Crowds remained

large and enthusiastic. His Royal Highness was in Canada to mark the sixtieth anniversary of Confederation. In Ottawa, August 4, before 25,000 people on Parliament Hill, with a choir singing "O Canada" and "God Save the King," he unveiled a statue of Sir Wilfrid Laurier and dedicated the memorial room of the Peace Tower. Sworn in as a member of the King's Privy Council for Canada, he announced that the King was replacing royal portraits destroyed in the 1916 fire.

This time his stay at the ranch was merely a holiday on a set royal progress. With him was his younger brother, Prince George. As mentor, Edward planned to introduce his sibling to the business of royal tours. Under Edward's guidance Prince George made his first public speech.

For the only time ever on a royal tour in Canada, the United Kingdom prime minister, Stanley Baldwin, accompanied the princes. This was ironic since within ten years Baldwin — a colourless person once described as cold mutton without mint sauce — was to be Edward's nemesis and architect of his abdication. It was almost as if Baldwin was hanging onto the coattails of Edward's popularity. In fact, Baldwin's politicking ended by upstaging him.

The tour lasted from July 30 to September 7, and started and ended in Quebec City. A highlight was the opening of the Peace Bridge at Niagara Falls, where the prince was joined by the American vice president, Charles Dawes. Dawes was put out by the tardiness of the prince's arrival, having been told by his security people that he was a sitting duck for a bomb attempt. To top things off, two stuffed seagulls with the American and Canadian flags had been placed at the centre of the bridge where the prince was to cut the ribbon, perplexing the royal party until they realized they were meant to represent doves.

A ball followed in Buffalo, New York. It was opened by the chief rabbi of that city. In Toronto the royal brothers inaugurated the Diamond Jubilee of Confederation Gates, giving them the popular name "Princes' Gates," which they have borne ever since.

The Prince of Wales was bored by official functions but loved parties. In Toronto he attended one in a house in Toronto's fashionable Rosedale, where he reportedly did a great deal of dancing. Miss Murdoch, gowned in sequined white with a beaded fringe, was his repeatedly chosen partner. Together they danced the prince's favourite Charleston. "According to the young people … it was a Charleston of his own — and, strange to say, an exceeding graceful one." By then quite a few young Canadian women could sing the popular song of that year: "I've danced with a man, who's danced with a girl, who's danced with the Prince of Wales."

"The 'impressive loyalty' of Canada is most impressive, and moves me very much," wrote Edward's assistant private secretary, Alan Lascelles, from Montreal at the end of the tour. "They sing 'God save the King' as if

Portrait of the Prince of Wales in Casa Loma's Peacock Alley, which His Royal Highness visited in Toronto.

1924 mural at Parkwood, Oshawa, Ontario, depicts the Prince (left) with the Orillia Hunt and its Master, Colonel R.S. McLaughlin.

The Prince of Wales greets United States vice-president, Charles G. Dawes, at the international boundary line, before cutting the ribbon to open the Peace Bridge at Niagara Falls, 1927.

it really was a prayer, and with their whole hearts in it … It makes one feel — particularly when at some western station you see a crowd of people who've ridden in forty or fifty miles just to get a glimpse of the two brothers — that there must be something worth working for in an institution which stirs a fine people so deeply."

The twenties gave way to the thirties, that low, dishonest decade. Depression and drought plagued the E.P. Ranch and all of Canada. The king's failing health precluded great tours, though the Prince of Wales's appetite for travel had also diminished. On January 20, 1936, he became King Edward VIII.

Vimy Ridge, near Arras, site of the bloody First World War conflict called Canada's battle of nationhood, is Canadian soil under French sovereignty, a gift from France to Canada. In his 325 days on the throne, Edward VIII carried out only one official function in a foreign country as king. It was the unveiling of Walter Allward's stupendous Vimy Memorial to honour Canadians who fought and died at Vimy Ridge.

As Canada's king, His Majesty inaugurated the monument July 26, 1936. Six thousand veterans and some 2,500 mothers, wives, and daughters of the fallen made the pilgrimage from Canada. Albert Lebrun, the president of France, was there too. After pulling aside the gigantic Canadian Red Ensign enveloping the gleaming stone structure, in a moving speech the king called the great monument "an inspired expression in stone." It marked, he said, "the scene of feats of arms which history will long remember, and Canada can never forget." After mingling and talking with the crowd, the king flew back to prepare for a veterans' garden party at Buckingham Palace.

"Today we meet under less solemn and certainly happier circumstances, although I am sorry to say somewhat damper circumstances," His Majesty joked in a brief address. *Canadians*: "We don't care. We are enjoying ourselves." *King*: "I don't take any responsibility for the rain. I can only hope you have not got wet, and when I know how badly the rain is needed in Canada, especially in the west." *Canadians*: "Alberta! High River!" *King*: "I can say that we certainly have the rain in the wrong place. I want to assure you what

King Louis XIV Canadian Royal Heritage Archives

This sensitive dry-point of "Our Beloved King," Edward VIII, by Ernest Fosbery, RCA, was commissioned by the Rolland Paper Company Limited of Quebec to mark the monarch's intended coronation.

a great pleasure it is to welcome you at Buckingham Palace, and to see you before you sail to your homes in Canada." *Canadians*: "For He's a Jolly Good Fellow …"

"Canada feels that he [Edward] is her own possession," noted the governor general, Lord Tweedsmuir, when Edward VIII's abdication a few months later shook the country. Canadians had had no inkling of their king's deep unhappiness. Not disturbed so much by Wallis Simpson's divorced state, the people of Canada did balk at the notion of an American as queen.

They felt let down by Prince Charming but they never turned on the Duke of Windsor, as Edward became. The Prince of Wales's work was remembered. Canadians showed this through the reception they gave the duke and duchess on their two post-abdication

King Louis XIV Canadian Royal Heritage Archives

"We raise this memorial to Canadian warriors," said King Edward VIII, addressing thousands of Canadians in France, before removing the huge Canadian Red Ensign draping the figure that symbolizes Canada and inaugurating the stupendous Vimy Ridge monument.

visits to the E.P. Ranch. The duke's old feeling that he was a Canadian had not changed either. His attempt to become governor general of Canada in 1945 proved it. He never could accept that having failed as king he was no longer in a position to make conditions.

After being unable to go to the E.P. Ranch in 1940 on his way to take up the governorship of the Bahamas, Edward succeeded the following year. But not without opposition; he had to journey through the Midwestern United States to reach Canada. Ottawa, fearing popular demonstrations, did not want him going by train through the three big cities of Montreal, Toronto, and Winnipeg. His Royal Highness and Her Grace the Duchess entered Canada September 28, 1941, at North Portal, Saskatchewan.

At the border, the duke was handed a letter of welcome from Mackenzie King, the prime minister, who had tried to stop him from coming. Edward telegraphed his thanks. When he and the duchess reached

King Louis XIV Canadian Royal Heritage Archives

Chief Morning Star, Banff, 1919.

Calgary the next day, the crowd greeting them was so large they had to put off a planned tour of the city.

Their stay lasted nine days. Edward at last showed the woman he loved, for whom he gave up Canada, the adored ranch of his youth. They drove to it through rain, mud, and swollen creeks. "I like it very much," the duchess said when asked her opinion of the E.P. The Windsors' stay was genuinely a period of rest and quiet for the couple.

Chiefs of the Stony Indians, who made the Prince of Wales Chief Morning Star in 1919, came to greet the duke. The duchess got together with local women. She refused to talk about clothes and told them about infant welfare projects in the Bahamas instead. Summoned back to Nassau after a hurricane struck the islands, the duke and duchess had to leave the ranch and Alberta prematurely. "Come back soon," crowds in Calgary who turned out for their departure called to them.

A planned visit to the ranch in 1945 had to be shelved because of wartime travel restrictions. The duke and duchess went on a fishing holiday to New Brunswick in July instead. But they arrived in Alberta again April 11, 1950. The duke denied to reporters that he planned to sell his ranch. "It is the only piece of property I've ever owned," he laughed wryly. He discussed his plans to replace his purebred shorthorns with a herd of Herefords.

The duke and duchess made the viceregal suite of the Palliser Hotel their headquarters. Furniture was brought from the Banff Spring Hotel to spruce it up. The E.P. had been nine years without an occupant. His Royal Highness was delighted to see it was less dilapidated than they expected, but it was not in shape for them to stay in. The duchess openly spoke of their plans to renovate the house. They would spend more time in it in the summer months she said, as a base for hunting and sightseeing.

The ranch was revitalized during the 1950s. At the Calgary Petroleum Club, where they lunched that second visit, the Duke of Windsor became the first to sign its guest book. The club president hoped he would "try again in the oil search [at the E.P. Ranch] and that discovery will be your reward." It never was.

Duke and Duchess of Windsor at the E.P. Ranch, September 1941.

Simon Evans in his study of the E.P. Ranch, *Prince Charming Goes West*, concludes that it was probably not the failure to make the property into a paying proposition or to find oil that finally led the Duke of Windsor to reluctantly sell it in 1962. The reason for its sale had more to do with the duke's health. By then he and the duchess had settled down to a comfortable way of life centred on the Bois de Boulogne in Paris. The E.P. was too far removed to be on their circuit.

Prince of Wales, King Edward VIII, Duke of Windsor — His Royal Highness had owned the E.P. Ranch for over forty years. In that period it had made an outstanding contribution to Alberta and Canada.

By 1962, regard for the impact of his actions on the monarchy was not uppermost in the duke's mind. Had it been, he might have seen that ownership of the now historic property by a member of the royal family would strengthen the crown in Canada.

As it was, a group of more perspicacious businessmen offered to buy the property for the duke's great-grandnephew, Prince Charles, the new Prince of Wales.

Prince of Wales in a panel of the great stained glass window marking the Silver Jubilee of King George V in 1935 at Toronto's St. James' Cathedral. His niece, Queen Elizabeth II, rededicated St. George's Chapel, which contains the window, July 4, 2010.

Arthur Bousfield

105

The Palace declined their imaginative and generous offer. Unlike refusing to send Prince Charles to school in Canada but later changing its mind and letting him go to Australia, its injudicious decision on the E.P. could not be rectified.

Chapter Eight

A PEOPLE'S KING

1913–1945

(King George VI)

EVENTS IN HISTORY ARE often described as "unforgettable," "historic," "seminal," or by similar effusive adjectives. Frequently the descriptions are exaggerated and readily forgotten by the next generation, if not sooner. Truly "unforgettable" events are marked by two qualities: they are remembered not merely by a compilation of facts but by anecdotal stories, and the stories are passed on from generation to generation until they become part of the identity of the community.

The royal tour of Canada in the spring of 1939 was a truly "unforgettable" occasion because it met those two qualifications in spades. King George VI, accompanied by his consort Queen Elizabeth, undertook the first tour of Canada and Newfoundland by the reigning monarch of those two (then separate) lands from May 17 until June 17. But, in fact, it was not the king's first trip to Canada and Newfoundland. Like his father, King George V, and his great-great-granduncle, King William IV, it was the Royal Navy that first brought George VI to Canada. The year was 1913 and Prince Albert, as King George VI was then known, was a midshipman aboard the cruiser HMS *Cumberland*.

Prince Albert was born on December 14, 1895, the thirty-fourth anniversary of the death of his great-grandfather Prince Albert, the Prince Consort and husband of Queen Victoria, after whom he was named. He was the second son of Prince George, Duke of York, and fourth in line to the throne. As a second son he was not expected to ascend the throne so a career in the navy was his future. Fate had other plans for Albert, as it had had for his father. Prince George of Wales was himself a second son but when his elder brother Prince Albert Victor, Duke of Clarence, died of pneumonia in 1892 he became Duke of York, then Prince of Wales in 1901, and King George V in 1910. Prince Albert of York took his father's former title of Duke of York in 1923 and then when his elder brother, King Edward VIII, abdicated in 1936 he became King George VI, taking his father's name as his own.

But all this was in the future when he became a cadet at the Royal Naval College, Osborne, in 1909 and subsequently at Dartmouth. On his ship's six-month training cruise in 1913 to Tenerife, the Caribbean, Canada, and Newfoundland, the royal prince received his introduction to royal tours in the

Historic picture of King George VI, in the uniform of a field marshal, and Queen Elizabeth taking the salute on the steps of the Centre Block of the parliament buildings in Ottawa.

In 1930–31 the prince almost returned to Canada. Now the Duke of York, married since 1923, and the father of two young princesses, Elizabeth born in 1926 and the newly arrived Margaret in 1930, he was requested as governor general by the Canadian government led by its new prime minister, Richard Bedford Bennett. The provisions of the Statute of Westminster had been worked out since the Imperial Conference of 1926, but the act itself was not passed until December 11, 1931. By its provisions Canada, and the other dominions, became equal realms with the United Kingdom under the sovereignty of a common king. The governor general was to be solely the representative of the king and not also of the British government and the appointment would be solely the concern of the king and the Canadian government. But months can be a lifetime and the new governor general would be appointed under the old rules, which gave the British government the right of final advice to the king. The Canadian government asked for the Duke of York. The British Secretary of State for the Dominions in the Labour government, J.H. Thomas, thinking he knew

Midshipman Prince Albert had the opportunity to visit Niagara Falls during his 1913 tour of Canada.

new world. As a seventeen-year-old he sometimes found the requests for social occasions too demanding and reportedly arranged for a look-alike fellow shipmate to occasionally stand in for him when he was not required to speak. Dances (with his commanding officer diplomatically ensuring an equal number of English and French Canadian girls as partners in Montreal) and sightseeing trips to Toronto and Niagara Falls were included in the itinerary. It left a fond memory with him of what would become his senior dominion.

A painting by Charles W. Simpson, R.C.A., depicts the arrival in Quebec City of the S.S. Empress of Australia *carrying the king and queen and escorted by ships of the Royal Canadian Navy and the Royal Navy.*

more about Canadians' attitudes than their own government, advised the king against the plan on the spurious argument that it would not work because Canada "was too close to the U.S.A. and the Canadians pride themselves as being as democratic as the Americans." Instead of having a third branch of the royal family reside at Rideau Hall, the distinguished, but non-royal Earl of Bessborough arrived in 1931.

So it was eight years later, in the spring of 1939 that King George VI came back to Canada. Arriving on the Canadian Pacific liner SS *Empress of Australia* and escorted by HMCS *Skeena* and *Saguenay*, one third of the tiny Royal Canadian Navy's fleet of six destroyers, and the Royal Navy cruisers HMS *Glasgow* and *Southampton*, His Majesty was two days late. Caught in a late season iceberg field, the ship had stopped for forty-eight hours rather than risk a disaster at sea. The

queen had written to Queen Mary, "We very nearly hit a berg the day before yesterday, and the poor captain was nearly demented because some kind cheerful people kept on reminding him that it was about here that the *Titanic* was struck and just about the same date!"

At the welcoming ceremony in Quebec City on May 17, William Lyon Mackenzie King, the prime minister, spoke for a Canadian people united in a common voice,

Today all the privy councillors of Canada have been invited to meet Your Majesty, including members of both present and past administrations. It is the first occasion since Confederation, apart from the meetings of the first cabinet, on which all members of the King's Privy Council for Canada have been brought together. It is

King George VI and Queen Elizabeth accompanied by William Lyon Mackenzie King, the prime minister, in full civil regalia, received Canadian privy councillors and their wives on their arrival at Quebec City.

the first time in the history of Canada that the ministers of the Crown, and indeed, all members of Your Majesty's Privy Council, have been assembled in the presence of their king. Today as never before the throne has become the centre of our national life.

Here, too, you will be in the heart of a family which is your own — a family of men and women of varied stock and race and thought, who in free association with other members of the Commonwealth, but equally in their own way, are working out their national destiny. We would have Your Majesties feel that in coming from the old land to the new you have but left one home to come to another; that we are all of one household … In our daily lives we see exemplified the things we value most — faith in God; concern for human well-being; consecration to the public service; delight in the simple joys of home and family life. Greater than our sense of the splendour of your state is our affection for two young people who bear in so high a spirit a responsibility unparalleled in the world

The tour started in the ancient capital of Quebec and then crossed and re-crossed the country by train, with occasional excursions to specific sites by automobile and occasionally by horse-drawn landaus. The major cities and towns on the itinerary included Quebec, Trois-Rivières, Montreal, Ottawa, Cornwall (reduced to a slow progression by the train rather than a stop to make up the two days lost from the tour), Morrisburg, Brockville, Kingston, Belleville, Toronto, Schreiber, Port Arthur and Fort William, Winnipeg, Brandon, Regina, Moose Jaw, Medicine Hat, Calgary, Banff, Kamloops, Vancouver, and Victoria, then back through New Westminster, Chilliwack, Jasper, Edmonton, Saskatoon, Melville, Sioux Lookout, Sudbury, Toronto again, Guelph, Kitchener, Stratford, Windsor, London, Ingersoll, Woodstock, Brantford, Hamilton, Saint Catharines, and Niagara Falls. After crossing into the United States for a three-day visit

the royal couple returned to Canada at Sherbrooke and continued on through Levis, Rivière-du-Loup, Newcastle, Fredericton, Fairville, Saint John, Moncton, Cape Tormentine, Charlottetown, Pictou, New Glasgow, and Halifax, then sailing to St. John's in Newfoundland. A map of Canada with the route laid out was engraved on the gold bowl that was the official gift from Canada to its king and queen.

The sheer number of stops on the tour made it historic, but the breadth only added to the more significant depth of the tour. Almost the entire population of the two dominions turned out in urban centres and at small railway crossings, often just to get a glimpse of the royal couple. British and American historians, with blinkered perspectives, have often characterized the tour as either an attempt by Britain to shore up Canadian support for the coming war with Germany or to reinforce a friendship and lay the groundwork for an alliance with the United States, or both. Undoubtedly the tour did both of those things but they were not the reasons for the tour. It was from first to last a Canadian initiative, fostered by

Outlook Cabin in Jasper Park provided a brief respite for the king and queen halfway through their arduous continental tour.
Toronto Star

the governor general, Lord Tweedsmuir, and the prime minister, William Lyon Mackenzie King. Tweedsmuir was a Scot, the biographer of Sir Walter Scott, and readily embraced and promoted the concept of a distinct Canadian monarchy, noting that a Canadian's first loyalty was "not to the British Commonwealth of Nations but to Canada and to Canada's king." Inspired by King George IV's tour of Scotland in the nineteenth century, organized by Sir Walter Scott to unite Scottish nationalism and royalism to the House of Hanover, Tweedsmuir sought to do the same for Canadian nationalism and royalism and the House of Windsor. Mackenzie King had a romantic attachment to the crown and the person of the king but was an anti-imperialist. A spiritualist, he held a séance on November 13, 1938, at which the late King George V appeared to tell him that the visit of the new king and queen was "due to their affection for you." This was coming out of Mackenzie King's own head of course but it clearly revealed how the prime minister viewed the trip. It was Tweedsmuir and King who organized the tour of Canada, not Whitehall or the White House, and neither was motivated by a primary desire to foster British interests per se. King insisted on accompanying the royal couple into the United States to emphasize that it was the Canadian prime minister, not the British prime minister, who was the king's senior adviser in North America.

The King of Canada takes his place on the throne of Canada for the royal assent ceremony, accompanied by the queen on the consort's throne, on May 19. It was the first occasion that a reigning monarch had been in the Canadian parliament and the first time a monarch had given royal assent in person in any Commonwealth parliament since early in the reign of Queen Victoria.

The king and queen's role in fostering the Canadian identity and their personal affection for all Canadians, not just Mackenzie King, would prove to be the defining elements of the progress of the tour as well as of its genesis and of its legacy.

When the king sat on the Canadian throne in the Senate chamber to give royal assent in person, something no monarch since Queen Victoria had even done in Britain, it gave life to the British North America Act and the desire of the Fathers of Confederation that the royal government of Canada should not only be carried out by the monarch's representative but also by the monarch in person. In his speech to the Senate and House of Commons he said, "It is my earnest hope that my present visit may give my Canadian people a

In Sudbury, Ontario, on June 5, the royal couple descended into the Frood mine properly attired in miners' helmets and raincoats.

deeper conception of their unity as a nation." When the queen laid the cornerstone of the new Supreme Court building, she noted that, "Woman's position in civilized society has depended upon the growth of law." Canadian newspapers crowed that with the king in the Canadian capital, Ottawa, not London, was for the duration of his stay the capital of the empire. May 20 was declared the king's official birthday and his Canadian household regiments, the Governor General's Foot Guards and the Canadian Grenadier Guards trooped the king's colour before their sovereign on the lawn of Parliament Hill to mark the occasion. At the banquet at Government House no toast was drunk to the king because Rideau Hall is the sovereign's home before it is the home of his or her representative so the king was the host. The king unveiled the war memorial "The Response" and declared that "the very soul of the nation is here revealed … Without freedom there can be no enduring peace, and without peace no enduring freedom." The king and queen grew as monarchs during their sojourn in Canada. That growth was what Canadians gave back to their sovereigns. A naturally shy man with a stutter, thrust into an unsought kingship through his brother's abdication, the king who arrived in Quebec on May 17 was unsure of his abilities and what he could offer his people. The

king who left St. John's on June 17 was a self-assured man. "The tour made us," the queen later explained.

Lord Tweedsmuir captured the other significance of the tour when he wrote to his sister after the royal walkabout in Ottawa, "It was a wonderful proof of what a people's king means." The plethora of anecdotes from the tour, repeated in books and conversations, passed down to future generations by those who were present, have become part of the folklore of Canadian history. There was the mayor of Montreal, Camillien Houde, with whom the king carried on his dinner conversation in both French and English. He forgot to wear his chain of office. The king noticed and asked him why he was not wearing it. Flustered, he blurted out, "I only wear it on special occasions." It has since been given apocryphal attribution to different mayors on various tours of Canada, as the story of the flustered mayor grew to mythic proportions in Canadian folklore. Even within the royal family the story had staying power. On the 1947 tour of South Africa, when dressing for gala events and deciding what to wear they would ask each other, "Is this a special occasion?"

In Winnipeg a tongue-tied local radio announcer tried to describe the arrival of the king and queen, accompanied by the prime minister, Mackenzie King, and greeted by the mayor, John Queen. Starting with,

In Ottawa King George VI unveiled the new war memorial, entitled "The Response," on May 21 before a throng of veterans and the public.

A.J. Casson painting of the royal procession passing the Canada Life building on University Avenue, Toronto.

The processional route to the provincial parliament building in Toronto, lined by soldiers and throngs of loyal spectators, was just one example of the huge crowds that turned out to welcome the king and queen to their Canadian home.

"The king, the queen and Mr. King have now arrived at city hall and Mr. Queen is on the steps to meet them"; he continued bravely through, "and now the king and Mr. Queen and the queen and Mr. King are moving into the reception hall"; but then lost all coherence as he floundered into, "now the king and Mr. Quing, I mean Mr. Keen and the quing … I'm sorry I mean … O sh —," while the audience listening in the square and on home radios roared with laughter.

In Levis the king arrived the day after the feast of Corpus Christi. The profuse decorations were left up to welcome the sovereign. A parishioner could still recall decades later how the parish priest in his sermon, the eve of the royal arrival, compared the presence of the king in his travels amongst his Canadian people as akin to the procession that day of the real presence

For the first time the Hudson's Bay Company in Winnipeg presented the king with the traditional tribute of two elk heads and two beaver pelts required by the company's royal charter whenever the monarch was present in the company's territory.

114

Woodbine Racetrack in Toronto was the scene of sporting pageantry as the king and queen arrived in a horse-drawn landau for the eightieth running of the King's Plate.

In Newcastle, New Brunswick, the king watched while the queen received one of the many bouquets of flowers presented to her on the tour.

The blue and silver royal train that carried the king and queen across the continent became the most recognizable symbol of the tour. This print of the train adorned the Victoria Day 1939 menu of the Prince Arthur Hotel in Prince Arthur, Ontario.

of Christ in the Host carried amongst the people in the Corpus Christi procession. Recalling his emotional departure from Halifax the following week, the king himself described the sentiment of the times, "I nearly cried at the end of my last speech in Canada, everyone round me was crying."

King George VI did not return to Canada after the 1939 tour. The Second World War followed within three months of his departure. In accordance with the Canadian independence His Majesty had embodied in the spring, on September 10, one week after he had declared war on Germany as King of the United Kingdom, at the request of the Canadian House of Commons, His Majesty declared war separately as King of Canada.

In the six years from 1939 to 1945, as in the First World War, much of the Canadian nation was in Europe fighting the war. The king and queen often

Above: *In Regina the royal couple left city hall through a guard of young Canadians.*

Right: *A colourful and distinctly Canadian decal was just one of innumerable souvenirs of the 1939 royal tour.*

WELCOME TO The KING AND QUEEN 1939

visited the Canadian troops in Britain and the king visited them in the front lines in Italy and France as his father had done a generation before. In Italy he bestowed the Victoria Cross on a Canadian officer, Major Paul Triquet of the Royal 22e Régiment.

A postwar tour was planned but the king's poor health made it impossible. In the fall of 1951 that tour was undertaken by the king's daughter and heir, Princess Elizabeth, who arrived in Canada with a draft accession declaration carried by her staff in the event the king should die during the tour. It did not happen but less than four months later, at the start of his daughter's tour to Australia, the king died at Sandringham on February 6 while the princess was in Kenya.

At Charlottetown's provincial legislative building the king signed the visitors' book. Prince Edward Island, named for his great-great-grandfather, was one of the provinces that the king had also visited in 1913 as a prince.

Toronto Telegram Collection, York University Archives and Special Collections

The tiny Royal Canadian Navy received the King's Colour from His Majesty during a ceremony on May 30, at Beacon Park in Victoria. In the war that would begin later that year the king's Canadian naval forces would grow to be the third largest in the world at the end of the conflict.

When asked for a general statement on the 1939 tour at its conclusion, Mackenzie King replied, "It speaks for itself. I don't believe anything I say could add to the story it has told." An eloquent expression of the tour's impact on Canadians was the plethora of commemoratives and souvenirs produced during and immediately after the tour of all fashions and qualities.

King George VI and Queen Elizabeth posed with their Royal Canadian Mounted Police escort on their final day in Canada.

From china and glassware to pins and tins, from programs to commemorative newspapers and magazines, many have survived into the twenty-first century.

Journalist Lotta Dempsey was giving birth to her son at St. Michael's Hospital in Toronto the day the king and queen arrived in the city. The nurse presented her with a white rose bud from a bouquet, saying, "Her Majesty has been sending bouquets presented to her to patients in hospitals and asked that this one especially be distributed to mothers of new babies, in memory of her visit and her own loved little daughters, Lillibet and Margaret Rose." Years later when taking a taxi to her son's home on his birthday she learned the driver was also born on the same day in 1939 at St. Michael's Hospital. His mother had died when he was a baby. After she told him the story of the day he was born, Lotta Dempsey concluded her account, "The driver pulled to a stop, turned around, and gazed at me with a strange and wondering look in the hard, narrowed eyes I had seen watching in the rear-view mirror. He said very, very softly, 'Then that's what the dried-up petals are in my mother's bible. I always wondered.'"

A first day cover marked the royal presence in Newfoundland, then not yet part of Canada, and the last stop on the royal tour.

When a memorial statue of the king was erected at Niagara Falls in 1963 its inscription reflected the nobility and humanity of King George VI that had touched those who saw him on the tour. It reads simply, "George VI King of Canada 1936–1952 A Very Gallant Gentleman." Although their number are now diminishing with the natural passage of time, another memorial of the 1939 tour is the way the eyes still light up and a smile still crosses the lips of Canadians who were there in 1939 when asked about the day they saw the king and queen.

On one of his many tours of his Canadian troops during the Second World War, this time in Italy, the king presented the Victoria Cross to Major Paul Triquet of the Royal 22e Régiment.

Chapter Nine

KHAKI GOVERNOR GENERAL

1901–1946

(Alexander, Earl of Athlone)

CANADA HAD BEEN AT war for nearly ten months when the Earl of Athlone, together with Princess Alice, arrived at Halifax, June 20, 1940, to begin his tour of duty as governor general. Canadian forces were overseas, including the first squadron of the Royal Canadian Air Force ever to leave Canada. France was falling; the commonwealth was on its own. Prospects were dismal but in his speech at his muted swearing-in at the senate on June 21, Athlone confidently reaffirmed his "strong belief in ultimate victory for the Allies and the restoration of peace in the world." War determined the style, tenor, and scope of the Athlone governor generalcy. Its world was khaki coloured. "The whole country threw itself into war work," Princess Alice later recalled. "It was very inspiring to be there at that time."

In the list of Canadian governors general, no royal nimbus aureoles the Earl of Athlone. His name, if anything, suggests one more distinguished peer among the many who represented the sovereign in Canada so long and so well. Yet Athlone's viceroyalty is rightly numbered as one of three Canadian ones held by the monarch's immediate kin. Canadians of

the day had no doubt that he was a member of the royal family.

George VI, the king who appointed Athlone to Ottawa, was his nephew. Queen Mary, the Queen Mother, was Athlone's sister. The siblings belonged to the royal house of the Kingdom of Württemberg, but an "unequal" marriage with a beautiful and tragic Hungarian countess had reduced their branch to morganatic status. Athlone's formidable mother, on the other hand, Her Royal Highness Princess Mary Adelaide of Cambridge, was a colourful member of the royal family. This good humoured, stout lady with a propensity for piling up debt as well as weight, was the daughter of the Prince Adolphus whose recollection caused a lonely Prince Edward to shed a tear on seeing a marionette of his brother in an eighteenth century Quebec theatre.

Athlone's royal affinity, obvious in his day, is concealed from us by his title. It hides the fact that he was born His Serene Highness Prince Alexander of Teck in 1874 and remained so until King George V made all the royal family give up their German titles in 1917, a move the young prince privately characterized as stupid, petty camouflage. Only at that point did

Robert McWilliams Collection

King Louis XIV Canadian Royal Heritage Archives

THE CITADEL
QUEBEC

Canada has entered the second year of the war with her decks cleared for action and with a grim determination to see that her sons overseas lack nothing that human ingenuity can provide in equipment and supplies and reinforcements. Our course is now set and I feel confident that if we are prepared for any sacrifice, we shall emerge from the storm with our flag still flying. Athlone.

Above: *Signed presentation portrait photographs of Her Royal Highness Princess Alice, Countess of Athlone, and His Excellency the Right Honourable the Earl of Athlone, governor general and commander-in-chief of Canada, show both in uniform. With Canadian society on war footing, their time at Government House was taken up with the manifold concerns of modern total war.*

Left: *Message to the Canadian people from Lord Athlone, December 1940, a few months after he took office.*

Alexander acquire the surname and peerage by which he is still known. The surname was Cambridge, from the dukedom that George III conferred on Adolphus, his seventh son and the grandfather of Alexander.

Prince Alexander took part in the 1901 tour of Canada by the future King George V and Queen Mary. On the train's return from the west he briefly got lost on a shooting expedition in Manitoba. A decade later, in May 1914, Prince Alexander's appointment as governor general of Canada was announced. He was to take office in October, but by then the First World War had broken out and was well on its annihilating and bloody course. The time of the current governor general, the Duke of Connaught, was accordingly extended.

A young Prince and Princess Alexander of Teck seen in June 1914, when His Serene Highness was governor general designate of Canada. Both were in the extended order of succession to the throne.

Alexander went to join the 7th Cavalry Brigade instead of going to Canada.

When he was reappointed to Canada twenty-six years later, Lord Athlone was thus not without Canadian experience. By then he had had a distinguished career. From 1923 to 1930 he was governor general of the Union of South Africa. It was a rough but productive school. His time there coincided with some of that country's most turbulent years, beset with bitter political and racial strife. Athlone performed so well and was such a popular viceroy that his time in the Union was prolonged.

Prince Alexander had other royal credentials too. In 1904 he married a vivacious young cousin, Her Royal Highness Princess Alice of Albany. Princess Alice was the only daughter of the ill-fated and by then long-deceased Prince Leopold, Duke of Albany. It was a love match and in the bride's background laid an

untold Canadian tale. In 1878, when Alice's aunt, luckless Princess Louise, arrived in Canada, she quickly discerned the crown's vulnerability in the vast country. With characteristic foresight and confidence Her Royal Highness offered a solution. "I think it possible you may come here one day," she wrote to her brother, Prince Leopold. "Canada is so loyal, so interesting, and with such a marvellous future that it really seems as if the governor generalship should always be filled by a member of our family."

When Leopold discovered Canada for himself a few years later, it touched his heart. Through no fault of his own, however, this talented and aesthetic prince was fated not to come to the country as governor

When reappointed to Canada in 1940, Lord Athlone had considerable experience as a leading royal family member.

general. Though he lobbied hard to obtain the vicere-gal appointment, he ran up against the more powerful influence of his mother, Queen Victoria. Her Majesty had been making use of Leopold as her secretary. She had no intention of foregoing so satisfactory an arrangement. The queen quickly thwarted her son's aspirations. Not long after, however, the hemophilic Leopold suffered the fall that caused his death from bleeding at the age of thirty. Nearly sixty years later the arrival of Leopold's only daughter, Princess Alice, at Rideau Hall as chatelaine was like the long delayed fulfillment of a cherished dream.

To have part of the monarch's family in wartime Ottawa was useful for Canada. Trained from birth to serve, Lord Athlone and Princess Alice were not only professionals. Their South African service as represen-tatives of the king meant they needed no on-the-job training. Talent, outlook, and character all suited them for the Canadian role. They were assured of success. "Am I too old?" was the first question Lord Athlone modestly asked Vincent Massey, Canadian high com-missioner in London, after the king told him Canada wanted him as governor general. Without hesitation Massey said no. Besides his well-known dedication to duty, Massey believed Athlone "shared his family's ability to come down by a sort of instinct on the right side of a public issue."

After Princess Alice put Rideau Hall in order and mastered every detail of its management ("She knew if a duster was misplaced" a staff member once said), the newly arrived Athlones began their initial round of visits to major cities and all provinces. First in 1940 were Halifax, Montreal, and Toronto. For their long trips throughout Canada, they used the beautiful 1939 royal-tour train, on which the governor general and his wife had two comfortable and elegant coaches. In reality, a residence by royalty is one perpetual tour, and the Athlones' journeys around Canada continued throughout their time in office.

Notes about the Athlones' 1941 visit to Winnipeg left by Roland McWilliams, who was Manitoba's lieu-tenant-governor for twelve years, and his wife Margaret McWilliams, give a glimpse of such trips. The Athlones'

Under the governor general's flag, Princess Alice took the salute at the Manitoba legislature, Winnipeg, April 1941. And in the brisk spring wind (causing Mrs. McWilliams, wife of the lieutenant-governor of Manitoba to hold her hat), inspected a Canadian Women's Auxiliary Corps contingent.
Robert McWilliams Collection

days in the provincial capital, April 24 and 25, on their return from British Columbia, coincided with a pro-vincial election that kept the premier busy on the cam-paign circuit. In the run up to the visit, the governor general and Princess Alice indicated that they wished to see "wartime activities" and have "as few social engagements as possible." Attire at the only dinner in Winnipeg would be "service dress" with "business dress" for civilians. Princess Alice thought it would be better "if she undertook an entirely separate programme in the afternoon and thus have an opportunity to visit various organizations in which women are engaged."

Included in the Winnipeg events were a luncheon for the governor general at Fort Osborne Barracks, a review of 2,000 active service troops, and time with the Air Service and Naval Volunteer Reserve. Despite the somber wartime garb for the Government House dinner for thirty, Her Royal Highness wore "a silver lamé gown with a floor length sash of soft green with

King Louis XIV Canadian Royal Heritage Archives

Princess Alice's parents, Their Royal Highnesses the Duke (Leopold) and Duchess (Helen) of Albany, had a short married life. Leopold, who sought to be governor general of Canada, died at thirty from hemophilia, a blood disorder thought to have been introduced into the royal family through a mutant gene in Queen Victoria.

shoes of the same shade" and "a diamond tiara." The thirty diners sat at two tables decorated with bowls of white lilies alternating with white candles, "producing a lovely effect against the black oak." At the end of the dinner, Princess Alice led the ladies from the dining room, "She and they curtseying to His Excellency as they left." The Winnipeg visit also included a reception at the parliament buildings, another at the city hall and the princess's speech to 450 at the Women's Canadian Club at the Fort Garry Hotel. At the parliament buildings Princess Alice also held a short reception for "six French Canadian and French women's organizations" who had only been "induced to work together" after "much difficulty and skill" and to whose address she replied in fluent French. On the lieutenant-governor's farewell call at the viceregal train, Mr. McWilliams recorded that "as we left the princess kissed Margaret."

The McWilliams' reaction to Lord Athlone and the princess was representative of the feeling they evoked in Canadians everywhere. "They proved very simple and unaffected people and quite easy to talk to, particularly the princess who was most friendly and vivacious," His Honour recorded, adding, "Her good looks, handsome clothes and charming manners delighted everybody."

Integrity and sound common sense were at the heart of the tall, balding Lord Athlone with his soldierly bearing and distinguished public manner. His great interest in people and places assured a good rapport with the public. On duty he was shy and modest but clearly amiable, friendly, and sincere. Against his tall imposing figure, Princess Alice was small and slender with pale colouring. As beautiful and fragile as Dresden china was how one observer described her. To Henry Willis-O'Connor, the chief aide-de-camp at Rideau Hall, she was "lovely to look at and easy to get along with." An extrovert with a sense of her own worth, Princess Alice was at the same time also known for steely determination, unflagging energy, keen intelligence, efficiency, a talent for putting people immediately at ease, the irresistible combination of friendliness and princely dignity, a hearty and infectious laugh, and skill at speech writing and making.

Though Lord Athlone, called Alge — pronounced Algie — by his wife, was subject to infrequent outbursts of temper usually provoked by trivialities, their marriage was a very happy one, a source of strength to both. They were suited for each other. Even the great tragedy of their lives — losing their only son Rupert who inherited the hemophilic gene and was killed in a car accident — only brought them closer together.

The March 1941 tour to British Columbia was a cross-country one taking the viceregal couple to Edmonton, Vancouver, and Victoria. At Fort William on Lake Superior they visited an airplane factory, the first one in Canada to employ women. Lord Athlone was made Chief Rainbow by the Ojibwas and he and the princess joined cheerfully in the Native dancing. On the prairies, His Excellency became the first governor general to visit a Mennonite village. In her memoirs *For My Grandchildren*, Princess Alice recalled that "In the school where there were pictures of Bertie [King George VI] and [Queen] Elizabeth on the walls, they sang *God save the King* and *O Canada*" and "We spoke German with the old folk." They returned east through Calgary and Regina. Twelve thousand schoolchildren paraded in the Saskatchewan capital "looking like a vast display of flowers." At every stop the princess's "keen eye looked for possible improvements in working and living conditions," which, with her frankness and candour, she never failed to point out.

In summer 1941, Lord Athlone and the princess made a tour of the Maritimes, visiting military camps "cut out of the forests" in New Brunswick. At Halifax "They had apparently mislaid the premier, but a stout man squeezed into a corner turned out to be he," Her Royal Highness remembered. President Roosevelt persuaded Lord Athlone to visit Alaska on his Pacific coast journey in autumn 1943. Alaska was a major supply point from which American tanks and arms were sent to the Soviet Union. To their hosts' amazement, Athlone and Princess Alice quickly established a far greater rapport with the Russians than the Americans were able to. The governor general drove on seventy miles of the new Alaska Highway, an all-weather 1,523 mile route from Dawson Creek to Fairbanks constructed as a military road at a cost of a hundred and fifty million dollars. Athlone also flew from Prince Rupert to Annette Island in a Catalina aircraft.

Focus of the tours was always the immense war effort Canada was putting forth, which was enormously expanding its industry. In speech after speech, Lord Athlone urged Canadians to strive harder to win the war. Their responsibility was, he said, to ensure "that each of our children and their children and all those who now suffer humiliation and defeat will be beholden to us for their salvation, their freedom and civilization." He and the princess visited every service establishment along their route. Princess Alice was

Lord Athlone inspecting a standard field piece manufactured at Sorel, Quebec, for the country's forces.

The princess in a new Canadian tank.

often in khaki too, wearing uniform to inspect what she called the "endless, endless war factories" or visiting the three women's services.

Lord Athlone's first year and a half as the king's representative coincided with the period before American entry into the Second World War. Bringing leadership and public opinion in the United States closer to co-operation with the Allies was an important objective for him. One of his first visits therefore was to President Franklin Roosevelt at his country house, Hyde Park. As governor general he welcomed Roosevelt to Ottawa in 1942 to address the Canadian parliament. Athlone was official host for the two international Quebec conferences in August 1943 and September 1944. When touring western Canada he wisely visited Seattle and Portland to inspect joint defences, as well as Canadian cities.

At one of the Quebec conferences Princess Alice ran afoul of "the president's toughs" as she called the security men surrounding Roosevelt. A G-man, sprawling on one of the sofas in the drawing room of the Citadel, forbade her from going to the terrace to welcome the president, until Winston Churchill rescued her. Athlone objected to the slovenly appearance of the shirt-sleeved security people who were to be posted on the landings of the stairs. He told their chief that he intended to station a Mountie in scarlet tunic beside each one, a threat that led to the quiet withdrawal of the G-Men.

Ever since the eighteenth century, Canadians had been asking to have their royalty in their midst. That wish was again achieved with the Athlones. Government House swarmed with royalties, major and minor, domestic and foreign, heightening the interest, excitement, and colour of a sometimes dull capital. Family joys, tensions, and sorrows were played out there. In August 1941, His Royal Highness Prince George the Duke of Kent, Athlone's nephew, made his first tour since 1927, when he had accompanied his eldest brother the Prince of Wales to Canada. Kent became the first member of the royal family to fly the Atlantic. His mission was to inspect Commonwealth Air Training Plan training centres scattered across the country, and other wartime

The most important member of the royal family to tour during the Athlones' time at Rideau Hall was their nephew, the Duke of Kent (Prince George), brother of King George VI. His Royal Highness is seen at government house in Winnipeg with Roland and Margaret McWilliams.

endeavours. Beneath Canada's enemy free skies, Canadians, British, Australians, South Africans, New Zealanders, and Americans trained as pilots under the Plan before going into combat overseas. Roland McWilliams, the Manitoba lieutenant-governor, was host to the duke at Winnipeg and found him "a most agreeable visitor, quite ready to adapt himself to whatever came up and not sticking on formalities."

A year passed before Lord Athlone and Princess Alice learned that their parting with the shy, charming, artistic young Kent, who spent his final days in Canada with them at the Citadel, had been the last. In April 1942, flying on an inspection mission to Iceland, His Royal Highness was killed when his plane unaccountably crashed in Scotland, leaving the royal family in shock. Plans that had been made for the evacuation of Athlone's sister, Queen Mary, and his

Above: *Lord Athlone and the princess photographed with King George II of the Hellenes (Greece) at Rideau Hall.*

Left: *Receiving foreign royalty cast up on Canada's shores by the ill fortunes of war. Princess Alice with Queen Wilhelmina of the Netherlands.*

At Montreal's Sun Life building, Her Royal Highness inspected reading matter destined for the troops overseas.

King Louis XIV Canadian Royal Heritage Archives

It was a joy for the Athlones to have their grandchildren live with them in Ottawa during the war. The children are from left: Richard, Elizabeth, and Anne Abel-Smith.

great-grandnieces the princesses Elizabeth (Elizabeth II) and Margaret, to Government House to escape the blitz went unrealized. Queen Mary refused to leave the United Kingdom. The king and queen, for the sake of wartime morale and family solidarity, decided to keep their daughters close to them.

Another worry the Athlones had was the discredited Duke of Windsor. In 1941 the duke visited the E.P., his ranch in Alberta, but the governor general and Princess Alice successfully kept him away from Ottawa. "Aunt Alice won't, and cannot from my point of view, receive *her*," King George VI wrote, referring to Wallis, the Duchess of Windsor.

Another royal family member at Rideau Hall provided an unwelcome moment of tragedy. Alastair, the new Duke of Connaught, who succeeded his grandfather the former governor general when the latter died at ninety-one, was made an extra ADC to Athlone. Described as a "likeable fellow," young Alastair was vague and forgetful, his thoughts seeming "fixed on faraway places." After returning home from an Ottawa party one bitter winter night, he had a seizure while opening his window at Government House and fell out. The next day he was found covered in snow, half frozen, and died on the way to the hospital. In his last year as governor general, Lord Athlone appointed another relative as ADC, his great-grandnephew, Viscount Lascelles, eldest son of the Princess Royal (Mary). Lascelles, a young guardsman, was a freed prisoner of war.

A week after Lord Athlone reached Ottawa in 1940, his daughter, Lady May Abel-Smith — born Princess May of Teck — and her three children, Richard, Anne, and Elizabeth, came to live with them. The Athlone grandchildren did part of their growing up in Canada and enlivened Government House, on one occasion with fireworks, in the process. Richard, a delightful child with a passion for gadgets, was sent to Trinity College School, Port Hope, his sisters to the Institut Jeanne d'Arc for their education. Princess Alice watched them acquire the "self-reliance natural to Canadian children."

There were also the foreign royalties. Some, such as King George II of the Hellenes (Greece) and young King Peter of Yugoslavia, were passing through Canada. Others, forced by war to leave Europe, took up residence for brief or longer periods. Queen Wilhelmina of the Netherlands, who came in 1942, was Princess Alice's formidable first cousin. Her laudable determination not to inconvenience her hosts in the end gave them more trouble than lack of consideration might have. Queen Wilhelmina's daughter, Crown Princess Juliana, remained in the Canadian capital for most of the war and her daughter, Princess Marguerite, was born there. Other royalties included the Grand Duchess of Luxemburg and Crown Princess Martha of Norway. Zita, the venerable former Empress of Austria and Queen of Hungary, with her numerous children, made her home in Quebec City. When entertaining these royalties at Rideau Hall, Princess Alice invariably set them to work making clothes for people bombed out in the London blitz.

Social life at Government House was suspended during the war but the conflict generated its own requirements, which the viceregal couple fully met. Princess Alice began giving popular tea dances for service personnel. At one, a young air force cadet who had danced frequently with Her Royal Highness asked the ADC on leaving, "Who was the precious white-haired lamb I've been rushing all afternoon? I've fallen for her in a big way." Besides the political and military figures involved in the direction of the war, people such as Charles de Gaulle, General Smuts, Madam Chiang Kai-shek, numerous movie stars, singers, and other performers promoting victory loans were entertained by

Despite wartime grimness, the viceregal couple enjoyed the pleasure of the Canadian winter. Tobogganing at Ottawa.

For My Grandchildren, Princess Alice

Skiing party at Camp Fortune, January 1943.

Archives Canada

Even in the year of victory, 1945, khaki dominated as Lord Athlone in uniform and Princess Alice walked to the senate chamber to open parliament, followed by the prime minister, William Lyon Mackenzie King.

Archives Canada

Planning Victory]

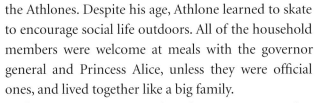

At Rideau Hall, the king's uncle, the Earl of Athlone, as governor general, confers an honorary degree on Franklin Delano Roosevelt, president of the United States.

Cover of National Film Board of Canada guide to the 1943 Quebec Conference shows Athlone as host to Roosevelt, Churchill, and King.

the Athlones. Despite his age, Athlone learned to skate to encourage social life outdoors. All of the household members were welcome at meals with the governor general and Princess Alice, unless they were official ones, and lived together like a big family.

"Prime Minister, you've been very naughty lately!" Lord Athlone would say, shaking his finger at Mackenzie King, the prime minister, whenever he caught the latter ignoring the governor general's constitutional right to be consulted, to encourage, and to warn. The populist Mackenzie King's ambivalent attitude towards the crown led to some friction but the consummate tact of both Lord Athlone and Princess Alice prevented a confrontation. It was at the Quebec conferences that Mackenzie King's resentment of the Athlones precedence over the prime minister irked him most. But their success in handling the touchy, insecure but crafty politician was such that on their departure they received a gushing letter from him stating that "Your years here as representative of the king

have strengthened the country's attachment to the crown. I doubt if that attachment were ever stronger than it is today." An example of Athlone's keen judgement was his summation of Mackenzie King years later as "A great man who just missed being quite a decent fellow."

Endearing anecdotes told about a member of the royal family are an indicator of the person's impact. Many stories are related about the Athlones. Despite his ability and excellent memory, the Earl of Athlone had a certain vagueness and often opened a subject to his ministers or aides without attaching a name or place to it. Guessing what he was talking about became an exercise in mental gymnastics. His intimates termed it playing Government House Dumb Crambo. Once, when crossing the prairies by train, Lord Athlone spotted a solitary house after miles of nothing. "Who lives there?" he asked. His aide rang the bell, a black attendant appeared. "I don't know, Your Excellency," the man answered when the question was

From the King's Bastion of the Citadel, Winston Churchill, the British prime minister, points out historic Quebec landmarks to Lord Athlone, Princess Alice, and United States Admiral William Leahy.

put to him. "Some son of a gun!" Several months later, a man from the west named Gunn was presented to the governor general. Lord Athlone smiled and said to the man, "I know where you live!" Another time he told his ADC in waiting that he wanted Edwards invited to lunch. Consultation with colleagues left the ADC still in doubt about who Edwards was. Three pairs of likely Edwardses were sent invitations in hope one would be the right one.

"We feel that we shall love Canada" Lord Athlone had said on becoming governor general. When he and Princess Alice left in March 1946, there was no doubt they had and that the tears shed by Her Royal Highness on departure were genuine. By then they knew enough about Canada to offer experienced advice. "Canada

Lord Athlone cuts the cake to mark the Royal Canadian Air Force's Silver Jubilee.

132

cannot be a nation," Princess Alice cautioned in her last speech, "unless Canadians have a national outlook. It is futile to sing *O Canada* unless the whole Dominion is signified and not just an individual province."

Athlone died in 1957 but the princess lived on nearly a quarter of a century longer and returned several times to Canada. At the 1981 memorial service for her in Ottawa, historian Jacques Monet, s.j., praised Princess Alice's leadership when at Rideau Hall. "On farms and in the cities, among industrial workers, at service clubs and at student rallies, with voluntary organizations and social circles, she sustained effort, comforted sorrows, kindled resolve, summoned courage, gave heart," he said.

Portrait of Princess Alice in later life. In 1959 the princess spent two months in Canada, staying at Rideau Hall where she admitted to General Vanier that "I find it difficult not to feel that I'm mistress here" because it seemed so much like home.

Chapter Ten

THE MAN WHO WILL BE KING

1970–2009

(Prince Charles, Prince of Wales)

THE PRINCE CHARLES, PRINCE of Wales, is the fourth Prince of Wales to have come to Canada. He has followed in the footsteps of his great-great-grandfather (Albert Edward), his great-grandfather (George) and his granduncle (Edward). He is also the only Prince of Wales to have toured with his spouse, having been accompanied by his first wife Diana, Princess of Wales, on three occasions and by his second wife, Camilla, Duchess of Cornwall, on his most recent.

Prince Charles was born on November 14, 1948, the first child of then Princess Elizabeth and the Duke of Edinburgh and second in line to the throne. He was created Prince of Wales in 1958 after his mother had become Queen in 1952. The ceremony of investiture at Caernarvon Castle in Wales took place on July 1, 1969, when the prince was twenty years old. The following year he began his personal involvement in Canadian life with the first of fourteen tours that have covered the following forty years.

The year 1970 was the one hundredth anniversary of the transfer of Rupert's Land from the jurisdiction of the Hudson's Bay Company to the Dominion of Canada and its rechristening as the Northwest Territories. Out of the land the new province of Manitoba was also created. To mark these centenaries the Queen and Duke of Edinburgh undertook a ten-day July tour of Ottawa, Manitoba, and the Northwest. The Prince of Wales and his sister Princess Anne accompanied their parents.

At the time of the 1970 tour he had declared that among the roles of a member of the royal family were "to be seen to be concerned" and "to exert some form of leadership."

A hallmark of the prince's tours has been the many speeches on a variety of subjects that he has delivered, and his willingness to poke fun at himself when he put his views out to the public to be embraced or challenged. On that first tour he gave an early example of how he would approach his duties, with a ditty he wrote and performed before the media accompanying him.

> Impossible, unapproachable, God only knows
> The light's always dreadful and he won't damn
> well pose,

Kenneth Woolley, Monarchy Canada Photo

Formal picture of HRH the Prince of Wales, as colonel-in-chief of the Royal Regiment of Canada, a Toronto-based reserve regiment, taken in Toronto in 1979.

Most maddening, most curious, he simply can't
    fail,
It's always the same with the old Prince of Wales.

Insistent, persistent, the press never end,
One day they will drive me right round the bend,
Recording, rephrasing every word that I say:
It's got to be news at the end of the day.

Disgraceful, most dangerous to share the same
    plane,
Denies me the chance to scratch and complain.
O where may I ask you is the Monarchy going
When princes and pressmen are in the same
    Boeing?

N.W.T. Government Photo

The Prince of Wales in the Northwest Territories (now Nunavut Territory) in 1970.

Five years passed before he returned to Canada, but 1975 would see Charles in the country on his own twice, for two very different purposes. In April there was a return to Ottawa and the Northwest Territories for an eleven-day solo tour. Then, from May 2 to June 5, he spent thirty-five days training with Canadian forces as part of a Royal Marines Commando contingent. On his 2009 tour he spoke of that earlier experience with

more than a touch of irony, "Remembering with fondness the time I spent back in 1975 on exercises with Her Majesty's Canadian Forces when I was serving in the Royal Navy and found myself in a tent for three weeks in a somewhat inaptly named place, called Blissville — near Gagetown military base in New Brunswick."

The month of training also included time in Nova Scotia and Montreal. It was followed by four tours to Canada in five years for the prince. The next year was the year of the Olympics in Montreal and Charles joined his entire family, together in Canada for the first time, for the sports extravaganza in which his sister was competing in the equestrian competition. But earlier that year, on February 18, the Prince of Wales came into Canadian homes in a different way. The Canadian Broadcasting Corporation presented a forty-minute television show on His Royal Highness, entitled *The Family Prince*. It featured an extended interview of the prince by the producer Jeanine Locke.

Commando training in New Brunswick for the Prince of Wales in 1975.

At a 1975 mock Commonwealth Conference in Ottawa, attended by sixty-six students, the Prince of Wales discussed his role in society and his definition of kingship as "to be seen to be concerned" and "to exert some form of leadership."

In July 1977 there was a short but significant trip to Alberta to mark the centenary of Treaty Number 7 between the Crown and the First Nations of Southern Alberta, at which he represented the Queen. In a tradition extending back to other members of his family in the nineteenth century, he was made a Kanai chief in the Blackfoot Confederacy and given the name Red Crow, borne originally by the nineteenth century chief of the Blood tribe. He was joined in Calgary for the Stampede by his brother Prince Andrew.

During the first week of April 1979 western Canada saw the prince once again. This time he visited Victoria, British Columbia; Winnipeg, Manitoba; Toronto and Ottawa in Ontario; and Yellowknife, Northwest Territories. From March 30 to April 3, 1980, the prince travelled to Ottawa, Vancouver, and Victoria.

The marriage of Lady Diana Spencer to the Prince of Wales in 1981 led to a change in the royal presence in Canada. The next decade saw the prince return three times accompanied by the Princess of Wales. When the royal engagement was announced a new development was introduced into Canadian practice. It is a requirement that the Queen announce to Her Majesty's Most Honourable Privy Council in London

The Prince of Wales joined Queen Elizabeth II, Prince Andrew, and Prince Edward on the Britannia *during the 1976 tour, which also saw them joined by the Duke of Edinburgh and Princess Anne.*

At the 1977 Calgary Stampede, the Prince of Wales was accompanied by his younger brother Prince Andrew.

her consent to the marriages of her children. For the first time the Queen decided to elevate her Canadian council to the same privilege. So on March 27, 1981, at a meeting of the Queen's Privy Council for Canada, the chief justice of Canada, as the deputy to the governor general, declared on behalf of Her Majesty The Queen "her consent to her Canadian Privy Council to the marriage of His Royal Highness the Prince of Wales to Lady Diana Spencer."

A brief stopover in Victoria in October 1982 was the Prince of Wales first return to Canada since his marriage. The purpose of the trip was to visit Pearson College in Victoria for the annual meeting of the International Council of the United World Colleges. It was not until the next year that the tour that Canadians were waiting for finally happened, the first tour by the Prince and Princess of Wales together.

From June 14 to July 1, 1983, the royal couple captivated Canadians in seven provinces on a tour in which the princess was clearly the star attraction. The itinerary took them to Nova Scotia and New Brunswick from June 14 to 19; Ontario and Quebec, June 20 to 22; Newfoundland, June 22 to 25; and Prince Edward Island, June 26 to 27. The tour concluded in Alberta, June 28 to July 1. The final day was not only Canada's birthday but also the birthday of the Princess of Wales. A massive birthday party at Edmonton's 60,000 seat Commonwealth Stadium was a suitable celebration.

The Nova Scotia portion of the tour included a visit to St. George's Anglican Church in Halifax, which was designed in the eighteenth century by His Royal Highness's ancestor Prince Edward, Duke of Kent. The Ottawa portion included a brief excursion on the Quebec side of the provincial border to Kingsmere, the former summer home of William Lyon Mackenzie King, noted for its historic collection of ruins.

The prince made a brief stopover in Ottawa on October 30, 1985. Then the following year the royal couple returned to Canada, this time to British Columbia, which had not been included in the 1983 tour. The particular occasion was the opening of Expo '86, the world exposition being held in Vancouver.

The tour lasted from April 30 to May 7, and included trips to Victoria, Vancouver, Prince George, Kelowna, Kamloops, and Nanaimo. The official dinner in Vancouver was attended by the leaders of all four Canadian political parties — the Progressive Conservative, Liberal, New Democratic, and Social Credit. "Only royalty, Sir, could bring unity out of the political diversity represented by the four of us," noted Brian Mulroney, the prime minister.

At the British Columbia Festival of the Arts in Prince George, the prince spoke about the importance of arts for people, noting that deep in the human soul is a reflection of the beauty and harmony of the universe and people have a duty to their children to

The Prince of Wales leads the staff and students of Pearson College on a walk in 1982.

A 1983 reception at Rideau Hall in Ottawa gave some distinguished Canadians an opportunity to meet the Prince and Princess of Wales on their first trip to Canada as a couple.

develop awareness of this. "We must strive … to make living into an art itself, although it will always remain a tremendous struggle."

The fall of 1991 saw what turned out to be the last tour by the Prince and Princess of Wales before their separation in 1992 and subsequent divorce. Unknown to the Canadians who greeted them the tensions in the

Canadian Forces Photo

The Prince of Wales's Canadian tours also included visits to Canadian Forces stationed abroad. On November 26, 1986, the prince visited the Canadian Airborne Regiment, escorted by the commanding officer, Colonel Goudreau, at their United Nations base in Cyprus.

royal marriage were already driving the prince and princess apart, but appearances were kept up for the tour.

The tour was entirely limited to Ontario but it included both the south and the north parts of the province. The official welcome was held in the northern city of Sudbury, not the provincial capital of Toronto, to highlight the importance of the north. In Sudbury the royal couple visited Science North and the Inco smelter. Toronto still received a major part of the tour itinerary and had its own official municipal welcome.

While the prince attended a Business Leaders Forum in the city and studied plans to address the polluted Don River, the princess took Prince William and Prince Harry, who had accompanied their parents to Canada for the first time, on a tour to Niagara Falls. At one point in the Toronto programme Karen Haslam, the provincial Minister of Culture and Communications, lost her shoe.

Jaki Stephenson, Monarchy Canada Photo

The Prince of Wales's characteristic wit brought a smile from the premier, William Bennett (seated), the Princess of Wales, and others in the crowd at the official welcome in Victoria, British Columbia, on April 30, 1986, at the start of the royal couple's tour.

Janet Huse, Monarchy Canada Photo

Accompanied by the Princess of Wales, Prince William, and Prince Harry, the Prince of Wales signs the historic bible at St. James' Anglican Cathedral in Toronto on October 27, 1991.

The prince picked it up and put it on her foot. "My gracious, my prince is handing me my shoe," the minister remarked. "Thank goodness it fits," the prince responded.

The Prince of Wales also became the fifth royal to be made an honorary bencher of the Law Society of Upper Canada, the provincial association of barristers. In his speech at the ceremony he referred to this situation by commenting:

> We could start a practice operating from a particularly salubrious office block in central London, a move which would send shivers down the spines of the law societies throughout the Commonwealth. We could litigate and mitigate, expostulate and adumbrate. Perhaps, ladies and gentlemen, even titillate. The possibilities are limitless but I have taken legal advice and ascertained that we could be prosecuted under the Trade Description Act. So my idle dream has come to naught.

The prince was also able to renew his relationship with the Royal Regiment of Canada, of which he is colonel-in-chief, at Fort York Armoury. Allan Sinclair, a veteran of the Dieppe raid in the Second World War, at which the regiment suffered massive casualties, said of the prince, "He is very articulate. He knew exactly where the Canadians were at Dieppe and he knew exactly what we did. But the nice thing was that he understood how lucky we were just to come back from Dieppe, and he had a nice quiet way of letting us know that we are still remembered."

When the tour moved on to Kingston, the prince spoke to convocation at historic Queen's University, and expressed his views of the evolution and achievements of Canadians in building a country:

141

Within the Canadian federal home there are many rooms, each with its own particular memories. That home has housed the Native aboriginal peoples, the two founding immigrant European communities, each with its language and culture, and generations of other immigrants which Canada has never ceased to welcome from all corners of the world.

All have survived under one roof, thanks to a steadfast commitment to peace, the rule of law and good government; to the traditions of parliamentary democracy and a constitutional monarchy all of which, I believe, have served the country well …

Other countries … look at the Canadian example with envy and admiration. There is a certain genius in the Canadian political culture which helps to explain the extraordinary resilience it has shown in dealing so constructively and for so long with the stress and strains of cultural and regional pluralism …

Other strengths, too, are associated with Canada's political culture: practicality, common sense, realism, tolerance, and a concern always to try to move forward by consensus …

The world, in brief, needs Canada … a federation which remains the envy of much of the world and holds out the prospect … of a great future built upon a most distinguished past.

After more than a decade of joint tours with the Princess of Wales, the Prince of Wales returned to Canada in 1996 for his first solo tour since their separation. It took place from April 23 to 29 and took the prince from Ottawa to Churchill, the northern port city of Manitoba, to open Canada's newest national park — Wapusk. Almost the whole population of 1,000 turned out in Churchill to greet him. Churchill is famous for its polar bears and beluga whales but the prince expressed his disappointment at a missed opportunity. "My only regret, as far as this morning was concerned, was that I — as usual — seem to have chosen the wrong time of year to come. Because there was not a single solitary sign of a

During his 1996 tour of Churchill, Manitoba, the Prince of Wales had the opportunity to inspect the historic Hudson's Bay Company fort.

polar bear or a beluga whale. And being Prince of Wales, I feel particularly responsible for them." The Manitoba tour also included events in the capital city of Winnipeg.

Several private engagements in Toronto with charities, including the Business Leaders Forum, the Business Council on National Issues, and the Canadian Youth Business Foundation, took place when the prince returned to eastern Canada, as did another visit with the men and women of the Royal Regiment. The City of Hamilton was celebrating its 150th anniversary and was rewarded with royal attendance at the ceremony.

The successful tour concluded in New Brunswick where the prince was able to visit heritage projects in Fredericton, the Eagle Forest Products Company in Miramichi, and the Village historique Acadien near Bathurst.

A private skiing holiday in British Columbia brought the Prince of Wales back in 1998; this time accompanied by his sons Prince William and Prince Harry, now nearly adults.

Although the prince had been to almost all parts of Canada in his many tours since 1970 he had never been to the province of Saskatchewan or the Yukon Territory. That oversight was ended in April 2001 with a six-day tour to those two regions. In an address to the Legislative Assembly in Regina, he used his presence in the province that is noted as the birthplace of medicare to speak of his views on alternative medicine, advocating an "integrated model of health care, taking into account the psychological and spiritual dimension of the human being as well as the physical."

Eight years passed before the prince was able to return again to his Canadian home. In 2009 the country's involvement in the war in Afghanistan had given people a renewed appreciation of the role of the armed forces and both the prince and the Canadian government decided to make the forces the focus of the tour. It began in St. John's, Newfoundland, continued to Toronto and Hamilton, then on to Victoria, and concluded in Ottawa. In St. John's the prince laid a wreath at the National War Memorial of the province, which had fought in the First World War as a separate dominion in the British Empire and Commonwealth. In Toronto there was a presentation of new colours to his two regiments — the Royal Regiment of Canada and the Toronto Scottish Regiment (Queen Elizabeth the Queen Mother's Own), the latter which he had taken over following the death of his grandmother, who had been their colonel-in-chief for nearly seven decades. In an extensive and moving speech he addressed not only the contributions of soldiers but also of their families and spoke as a father as well as a prince.

As we gather to celebrate this special occasion, we remember generations past and the immense courage, service and sacrifice shown by your forebears over more than a century.

Embroidered onto each of the colours that I have presented to you are names familiar to us

The Prince of Wales, colonel-in-chief of the Royal Regiment of Canada, arrived at the Fort York Armoury in Toronto for a regimental gathering on April 27, 1996.

Lisa Mitchell, Monarchy Canada Photo

March 1998 saw the Prince of Wales, accompanied by Prince William and Prince Harry, take to the slopes of Whistler, British Columbia.

Lynne Bell, Monarchy Canada Photo

all: Vimy, the Somme, Passchendaele, Dieppe, the Rhineland; names which remind us of the horror and carnage of the First World War; the violence and bloodshed of the long and costly advance to defeat the Nazis and, of course, the extraordinary loyalty, bravery and resilience of Canadian soldiers who fought shoulder to shoulder with their Commonwealth brethren, for crown and country, many thousands of miles from their homes.

Today, both of your regiments continue in the finest traditions of your predecessors, only this time you have been deployed to other regions of the world, including the Golan Heights and Sudan and, of course, Afghanistan. I know that during the last two years, between your two regiments, you have provided forty-three soldiers for operations in Afghanistan who have worked in the most difficult and dangerous of environments in Helmand and Kandahar, often under the constant threat of direct and indirect attack. I can only begin to imagine how incredibly challenging and difficult it must be to operate in such austere, unfamiliar and hostile conditions. Miraculously, no one from your regiments has been killed. I am, however, aware that two of your soldiers were injured in Afghanistan and I am so relieved to hear that they have both made a full recovery.

As a father of two serving officers, one of whom has himself served in Afghanistan, and colonel-in-chief of twenty-two regiments, seven of which are Canadian, I have at least some understanding of the immense challenges faced by the families of those serving in the Canadian Forces and I can so well appreciate the appalling emotional strain and anxiety which permeates every waking minute while a loved one is placed in harm's way. To the families here this evening and, indeed, to all the families of the Canadian forces, I would like to express my deep gratitude for the unwavering support you have given to your sons and daughters, your brothers and sisters, your fathers and mothers, your husbands, wives and partners who serve in this great nation's armed forces. Your love, compassion and loyalty are an essential ingredient for a successful mission.

As you march off with your new colours flying, please be aware of your colonel-in-chief's undying interest and concern in all you do — but, above all, of the pride I feel in being associated with two such special regiments. God bless and preserve you all.

In Victoria the prince wore his uniform as a recently appointed honorary vice-admiral in the Canadian Forces to preside at celebrations anticipating the 2010 observance of the one hundredth anniversary of the Royal Canadian Navy. The tour concluded in Ottawa on November 11, where the prince, wearing the uniform of a Canadian lieutenant-general, participated in the annual national Remembrance Day observance at the National War Memorial unveiled by his grandfather in 1939.

The 2009 tour also brought a new dimension to royal tours. The Prince of Wales' second wife, Camilla, Duchess of Cornwall, whom he married in 2005, is the great-great-great-granddaughter of Sir Allan MacNab, the pre-Confederation Prime Minister of the Province of Canada. It was a chance for a member of the royal family to come to Canada and visit an ancestral home, Dundurn Castle, built by MacNab in Hamilton.

Since 1970 the Prince of Wales has challenged Canadians to think about their role, as individuals and as a country, in the world. During some periods his returns to Canada were frequent and in other periods several years elapsed between his sojourns. As the heir to the throne he has successfully navigated the fine line between the restrictions inherent in his status as the future monarch and the current freedom that he is not yet constitutionally bound by ministerial advice in making his interventions. As the Prince of Wales, the man who will be king, he is now second in longevity only to his great-great-grandfather King Edward VII.

Canadian Forces Photo

An honorary vice-admiral of Canada's Maritime Command, the Prince of Wales inspected a guard of honour at celebrations marking the hundredth anniversary of the Royal Canadian Navy at Esquimalt, British Columbia, November 2009.

Chapter Eleven

CANADA'S MOST VALUABLE PLAYER

1951–2010

(Queen Elizabeth II)

"IT IS VERY GOOD to be home."

With those words, Queen Elizabeth II concluded her opening speech at Halifax, at the start of her 2010 tour and residence in Canada. It was officially described as Her Majesty's twenty-second tour, but there were also her tour as princess, ten brief stopovers during the reign, a visit to Vimy Ridge in 2007 — which is Canadian soil under French sovereignty — and tours of Canadian war cemeteries in Normandy.

The queen's remarks were not merely a turn of phrase. Canada is, and has been, her home, both personally and in the context of eight generations of her family — five before her own and two younger generations. Her remarks alluded to a comment made by her mother, Queen Elizabeth, who said that "Canada felt like a home away from home for the Queen of Canada." Elizabeth II added, "I am delighted to report that it still does."

Elizabeth II's British biographer, Elizabeth Longford, has written that the queen "feels Canadian as well as being Queen of Canada, partly because she has been all over it." This sentiment started early. In 1951 Princess Elizabeth said, "From the moment when I first set foot on Canadian soil the feeling of strangeness went, for I knew myself to be not only amongst friends, but amongst fellow countrymen." Near the conclusion of that first tour she reiterated the feeling, noting that "In almost every mile that we have travelled through fields, forests, prairies and mountains we have been welcomed with a warmth of heart that has made us feel how truly we belong to Canada."

The queen has repeated the sentiment at various times in her life. In 1977 she added references to her ancestors, "My family's association with this country over many generations allows me to see and to appreciate Canada from another viewpoint, that of history." In 1978 she alluded to the fact that her bond with Canadians was a constantly growing one, "I am getting to know our country rather well." And in 1983, when leaving California for British Columbia, she casually remarked to an American that, "I'm going home to Canada tomorrow."

Queen Elizabeth II has been in Canada so frequently that it is not possible to give a complete description of each tour in the confines of this book. A summary of the residences and their highlights follows:

National Film Board of Canada

The entire immediate royal family gathered together in Canada for the first time at Bromont, Quebec, during the 1976 Olympics tour.

1951 — coast-to-coast tour as Princess Elizabeth;

1957 — first monarch to open parliament in Ottawa;

1959 — first coast-to-coast tour as Queen, including a visit to the Yukon Territory;

1964 — centenary of Charlottetown Conference, Prince Edward Island, Quebec, Ottawa;

1967 — presided at centenary of Confederation, Ottawa; Expo '67 in Montreal;

1970 — tour of Northwest Territories and Manitoba;

1971 — tour of British Columbia for its centenary;

1973 — twice: tour of Ontario, Prince Edward Island, Saskatchewan, Alberta; returned for stay in Ottawa for Commonwealth Conference in summer;

1976 — Nova Scotia, New Brunswick, Quebec, and Ontario for the summer Olympics;

1977 — celebrated her Silver Jubilee in Ottawa;

1978 — Newfoundland, Saskatchewan, and Alberta for the Commonwealth Games;

1982 — stay in Ottawa for patriation of the Canadian constitution;

In a scene that was to be repeated countless times in the queen's life, a young girl offered Princess Elizabeth flowers at a Winnipeg dinner in 1951.

Robert McWilliams Collection

1983 — tour of southern British Columbia;

1984 — New Brunswick and Ontario bicentenaries, Manitoba;

1987 — British Columbia, Saskatchewan, Quebec;

1990 — Alberta, Ottawa for Canada Day;

1992 — Ottawa for Canada Day;

1994 — Nova Scotia, British Columbia, Northwest Territories;

1997 — Newfoundland (500th anniversary of

The queen and the Duke of Edinburgh presided at the rededication of the Vimy Ridge Memorial in 2007, located on Canadian soil within France.

The first tour of Canada by Queen Elizabeth II, as Princess Elizabeth, and the Duke of Edinburgh in 1951 was marked in many different ways. One was this sheet music to a song composed in their honour by Fred Evis.

Caboto's Landing), Ontario, and Ottawa for Canada Day;

2002 — Golden Jubilee tour of Nunavut, British Columbia, Manitoba, Ontario, New Brunswick, Ottawa;

2005 — centenaries of Saskatchewan and Alberta;

2007 — rededication of Vimy Ridge memorial;

2010 — Nova Scotia for one hundredth anniversary of Royal Canadian Navy, Ottawa, Winnipeg, Toronto, Waterloo.

During her reign the queen also had ten stopovers in Canada, usually at Gander, Newfoundland, to refuel the plane — before the era of non-stop travel — taking her to other locations. Although these were brief stays lasting only a few hours, the queen sometimes undertook royal duties in the time allowed. Her first stopover at Gander, Newfoundland, on November 23, 1953, was actually her first time in Canada as sovereign, almost four years before her first official residence in 1957. She said, "It's nice to be in Canada again (referring to her earlier tour in 1951 as a princess), even if only for a short stay."

The full list of stopovers is as follows:

1953 — Gander, Newfoundland;

1963 — Edmonton and Montreal, two in Vancouver;

1974 — held investiture at CFB Uplands, Ottawa;

1974 — Gander, Newfoundland;

1985 — Gander, Newfoundland;

1986 — Gander, Newfoundland;

1991 — Gander, Newfoundland.

Queen Elizabeth II's presence in Ottawa on July 1, 2010, tripled the usual attendance at Canada Day celebrations, bringing the number of people on Parliament Hill close to 100,000. Wearing Canadian white and red and a diamond maple leaf brooch, the queen, "the head in our heads and tails" as journalist Joe O'Connor described her, arrived in the state landau, escorted by Mounties. Throughout the 2010 tour, Her Majesty seemed to bring out an unsuspected eloquence in the usually more plain-spoken prime minister, Stephen Harper. On the hill he welcomed her home and said Canadians should be proud of their history and heritage.

During the ceremonies the queen listened to a video of Brigadier General Jon Vance, thanking her for the personal message she sent to the Canadian Forces in Kandahar, which was viewed by them on Canada Day. Addressing her "fellow Canadians" in a five minute speech, the eighty-four-year-old queen pointed out the undeniable but seemingly impossible fact that she had been a witness to Canada for more than half its life since confederation. Praising the country for its dedication "to being a caring home for its own, a sanctuary for others," mentioning the Vancouver Olympics and Canada's servicemen and women, diplomats, and humanitarian workers who have earned "the respect of us all," Her Majesty concluded with the words, "God bless you all, and God bless Canada."

One of the most moving moments of the Canada Day noon show program was veteran actor Christopher Plummer's tribute to the sovereign. Referring to her as "the most travelled monarch in all history," he said she had "managed to keep royalty and the idea of royalty as something that is most attractive and comfortable to us, as she carried it with her well into the twenty-first century."

* * *

Thirteen of the queen's Canadian stays during her reign stand out for national events of pre-eminence. Acts of sovereignty, openings of parliament, addresses to the nation, privy council meetings, investitures, state banquets, celebrations of national occasions, attendance at milestone anniversaries — all these accompaniments of royal tours constitute what Jason Kenney, minister of Citizenship and Immigration, has termed the civic liturgy of Canada. When they involve the sovereign in person they achieve their maximum significance and effect.

Queen Elizabeth II attends the meeting of her Canadian cabinet, (a committee of the Queen's Privy Council for Canada), Government House, 1957. Prince Philip, who was sworn in on this occasion, is now the second longest serving Canadian Privy Councillor.

The most symbolic and splendid of Her Majesty's national occasions was in 1957. That year, for five days over the Thanksgiving holiday, October 12 to 16, the young monarch infused her capital of Ottawa with vitality, purpose, and pageantry. Four years before, all Elizabeth II's realms took part together in her coronation. Following her sacring and crowning, Her Majesty symbolically manifested her sovereignty as queen individually in each of her realms. The Canadian autumn weekend brought this global round to completion.

That Thanksgiving the queen made Canadian royal history. She became the first sovereign to open the Parliament of Canada in person. Vast numbers converged

The queen receiving the royal salute at the entrance to the parliament buildings, Ottawa, October 14, 1957.

"I greet you as your queen," Her Majesty tells senators and MPs. "Together we constitute the Parliament of Canada."

Processing through the rotunda, the royal procession makes its stately way to the Senate chamber for the opening of parliament.

on Ottawa for the event. Beforehand, on Monday morning, October 14, Her Majesty presided at a cabinet meeting at Rideau Hall. When John Diefenbaker presented an order-in-council for her signature, the queen gently corrected the new and inexperienced prime minister. "I usually just initial these orders-in-council," she said, before writing ER on the document. At 2:55 p.m., she and the duke drove in state to Parliament Hill, arriving just as emergency technicians got the lights fused by overloaded circuits working again.

A setting within a setting, the historic parliament buildings were the venue for the splendid but simple ceremony. Their majestic gothic architecture, a mute reminder of the royal character of Canada, was framed by the hushed glory of the Canadian autumn. In her coronation dress, the most gorgeous dress ever made for the queen, embroidered with the historic emblems of the crown including the maple leaf, Her Majesty processed with silent dignity to the senate, attended by the Duke of Edinburgh, the prime minister, and the great officers of parliament. "I greet you as your Queen," the sovereign declared to senators and members of parliament from the throne. "Together we constitute the Parliament of Canada."

This first parliamentary opening by the monarch had been envisaged by the Fathers of Confederation. The government of the new Canada, according to the Confederation Resolutions, was to be carried on "by the sovereign in person or by the governor general duly authorized." The royal opening, more elaborate and detailed on account of being performed by the queen, demonstrated the mediaeval roots of the Canadian constitution as well as its evolutionary nature. The order of the stately royal procession in parliament was laid down in 1399, but the content of her throne speech was 1957. In it, Elizabeth II set out her hope for her reign. "Though God hath raised me high," she said, quoting her famous predecessor and collateral ancestor the great Elizabeth I, "yet this I count the glory of my crown, that I have reigned with your loves." Then in her own words she added, "I say to you that it is my wish that in the years before me I may so reign in Canada and be so remembered."

The queen's Thanksgiving Day television address to the people of Canada that Sunday night was her first TV broadcast. When complimented on it, she replied modestly, "My husband is my producer," giving Prince Philip credit for her success. "I feel proud and happy," the monarch said, contemplating Canada in all its diversity, "to be queen of such a nation." The queen's pale green satin dress, appliquéd with dark green velvet maple leaves, enhanced the national character of the state dinner at Rideau Hall that followed the opening. Continuing the theme of sovereignty, Her Majesty left Canada for the United States on October 16. With John Diefenbaker as minister in attendance at her official visit to Washington, her presence there as Queen of Canada was made clear. Before leaving the Canadian capital, the queen said, "When you hear or read about the events in Washington and other places, I want you to reflect that it is the Queen of Canada and her husband who are concerned in them."

Wearing the famous maple leaf dress, Elizabeth II received her guests at the state dinner at Rideau Hall after opening parliament. The dress now belongs to the Museum of Civilization, Ottawa.

First day cover marking 1957 royal tour.

Above: *Following her 1957 stay in Ottawa, Her Majesty addressed the United Nations in New York. Fifty-three years later, after the 2010 Canadian tour, the queen spoke to the U.N. General Assembly for the second time in her reign.*

Top right: *Cover design from The Illustrated London News 1959 royal tour souvenir issue.*

Bottom right: *Ontario Department of Travel and Publicity souvenir of the seaway opening. Her Majesty spent fourteen days of her tour in Ontario. The seaway greatly expanded hydro electric power generation.*

King Louis XIV Canadian Royal Heritage Archives

"This occasion deserves a place in history." Elizabeth II, with President and Mrs. Eisenhower on her left — viewer's right — declares the St. Lawrence Seaway open, June 26, 1959.

At the international boundary, the queen unveiled a commemorative stone. Seen with the sovereign are U.S. Vice President Richard Nixon and his wife.

Royal Yacht Britannia making its way through the seaway.

Arrival of Queen Elizabeth II for the special outdoor joint centennial session of Parliament, Ottawa, July 1, 1967.

Two years later, in 1959, a pregnant Queen Elizabeth II — her condition then unknown to the Canadian public — carried out an 18,000 mile national tour in just over six weeks. The focal point of the journey was the joint ceremonial opening of the newly completed St. Lawrence Seaway on June 26, by Her Majesty as Queen of Canada and the president of the United States, Dwight Eisenhower. "One of the outstanding engineering accomplishments of modern times," the queen in her speech described the seaway that opened up the Great Lakes to ocean shipping. "This day," she concluded, "deserves a place in history." Adding to the glamour of the tour was the royal yacht *Britannia*. The queen and Duke of Edinburgh, to the accompaniment of church bells, sirens, and whistles of ships and boats, sailed from Montreal all the way to Port Arthur (Thunder Bay). Their route through the thousand islands to Ontario was the same one followed by the queen's great-great-great-grandfather, Prince Edward, to pioneer Upper Canada in 1792, 167 years before.

A blend of the official and the ordinary, the gala and the informal, the tour saw the queen in Ottawa to preside at the first of seven Dominion Day/Canada Day celebrations to date. As she would on July 1, 1967, 1973, 1990, 1992, 1997, and 2010, she offered words of praise, encouragement, solidarity, and hope to Canadians everywhere. "If I have helped you feel proud of being Canadian" she told them, "I shall feel well satisfied because I believe with all conviction that this country can look to a glorious future."

At the federal-provincial state banquet in Halifax at the end of the tour, Her Majesty announced the appointment of the new governor general, General Georges Vanier.

One of the greatest national celebrations of the Canadian polity that the queen ever presided over took place in 1967 — the centenary of confederation. National feeling, stimulated by the maple leaf flag that Elizabeth II proclaimed in 1965, had reached fever pitch. Less than three years earlier the rival nationalism in the country — French Canadian separatism

— had been experienced by Her Majesty. The risks inherent in nationalism were brought home to her when the violence of 1964 was seized as a pretext by some English Canadian nationalists, whose object was to divorce Canada from its roots, to blame the crown for the existence of the separatist threat. In that climate, Her Majesty's 1967 tour was a security-tight operation restricted to six days by an edgy federal government, far less time than was warranted by the occasion, and confined to the Ottawa region: Cornwall, Kingston, and Montreal.

Such confinement did not prevent the queen from being the highlight of the centennial festivities. In an editorial, the *Globe and Mail* called Her Majesty "The living symbol of our heritage, both English and French." The fifty thousand Canadians who turned out to see the queen on Parliament Hill agreed.

Her Majesty addressed senators and members in a joint session of both houses of parliament. It was held outdoors on the lawn of the hill, complete with speakers and maces, in the blazing summer sun. The

Reception during 1967 centennial celebrations.

Cutting the giant cake marking a hundred years of Canadian confederation.

Impromptu ride on the minirail at Expo '67.

Royal Visit
Canada 67

1967 royal tour first day cover.

queen radiated her simple dignity and grace. "It is altogether right and fitting that sovereign and people should meet together here at the heart and centre of Canadian existence to give thanks on this great occasion," Her Majesty said in an emotion-charged speech. She paid special tribute to "the ordinary people of Canada, who have given flesh and sinew to the plans of the Fathers of Confederation." A gigantic birthday cake decorated with her royal arms of Canada and the shields of the provinces and territories was cut by Her

Majesty. During the centenary, the sovereign presided at a meeting of the Privy Council for the swearing-in of nine provincial premiers.

The next day Her Majesty and the duke went by car to Kingston, accompanied by Lester Pearson, her third Canadian prime minister. Boarding *Britannia* there, they sailed downriver overnight in heavy rain to Montreal for Expo '67. Prince Philip had complained about the excessively heavy security restrictions so it was decided that Her Majesty could risk an impromptu ride on the minirail. As the queen boarded the rain stopped and the sun broke out. Cheers and shouts of "Vive la reine!" came from the jam-packed crowd as the little train made its way throughout the Expo site. A newspaper usually hostile to the monarchy grudgingly admitted that it was "One of the most royal triumphs" on any of the queen's tours. "The queen salvaged Quebec's honour," declared *Montréal-Matin*.

By the seventies, the queen was familiar with the paradoxes of her reign in Canada. Up to 1939, though the monarch had only toured the country prior to ascending the throne, Canadians found no difficulty seeing their sovereign as head of Canadian society. Now, when the queen was present to a previously undreamt of degree, a segment of opinion refused to accept her as Canadian because she was shared with other countries. They worked to end her institutional presence.

Two groups sought to repudiate the country's history and identity. One aimed to republicanize it, the other to carve a new ethnicity-based state out of it. Both correctly saw the queen as an obstacle to their plans. But wiser heads realized that legitimate national aspirations could be accommodated under the crown. The Queen's leadership was essential to prevent a disconnect with the historical identity of Canada.

Her Majesty's 1970 tour of the north had national significance from its obvious, if unadmitted objective of proclaiming Canadian sovereignty there. June 25 to July 5, 1973, was the queen's next major tour of national importance. The three-province journey, which Pierre Trudeau, the sovereign's fourth Canadian prime minister, was accused of having arranged to raise his sagging political fortunes, marked the centenary of

Post office first day cover for the Commonwealth government leaders meeting in Ottawa, for which the queen made her second stay in 1973 in the capital.

Prince Edward Island's entry into Confederation. The tour saw the queen preside at her third Dominion Day (Canada Day). Appropriately, this time the celebration was not in Ottawa but Charlottetown. However, what captured national attention in 1973 was the queen's speech at the state dinner for 1,400 held at Toronto's Royal York Hotel. Multiculturalism, a fact from the beginning of Canada, had been made a government policy, generating controversy. The sovereign let Canadians know how multiculturalism was regarded at the apex of society. "I am here as Queen of Canada and all Canadians — not just one or two ancestral strains," she said. "I want the crown to be seen as a symbol of national sovereignty belonging to all. It is not only a link between Commonwealth nations, but between Canadian citizens of every national origin and ancestry."

The queen's second stay in 1973 was in Ottawa from July 31 to August 4, for the Commonwealth heads of government meeting. Someone said the queen's presence made Ottawa "a real capital." Her Majesty received the world leaders in her dual capacity as Queen of Canada and Head of the Commonwealth. She found time for special Canadian duties too. She invested Roland Michener, who was about to retire as governor general, with the rarely given Royal Victoria Chain, and Jules Léger, soon to be appointed to the viceregal office, with the Order of Canada. She also received Canadian VC holders in the Hall of Honour in the parliament buildings.

In 1977 she was in Ottawa for the Canadian celebration of her Silver Jubilee. Wearing a white silk dress with a long gold French lace fringe, suggestive of Canadian native dress, and a diamond tiara that belonged to her grandmother, Queen Mary, Her Majesty opened the third session of the thirtieth parliament, October 16. It was a colder autumn day than the one in 1957. She told parliamentarians that a generation of Canadians had grown up during her twenty-five year reign. She felt "a special interest in these young men and women, contemporaries of our own children." With the country rife with constitutional turmoil, it was a time of great decision for Canada. A period "for rediscovering the strength and potential of Canadian society." And it would require "that Canadians rededicate themselves to each other's well-being just as I dedicate myself anew to the people and the nation I am proud to serve."

The next year, shock, anger, fear, and heated debate erupted when the government introduced a bill to remove the queen from Canada's internal constitution. Popular reaction produced an alliance of provincial premiers, including Quebec. They forced the dropping of all proposed changes to the crown. On April 17, 1982, a cold, sleety early spring day, the queen signed the proclamation of the Constitution Act, bringing the new amending formula and charter of rights into effect. The Act ensured that her royal role was not only intact but entrenched. Commentators were amused by the fact that the queen, as no one else could, saved the

The Queen of Canada and her government. Governor general, prime minister (Pierre Trudeau), lieutenant governors, and provincial premiers dined with their sovereign at a state dinner given by the queen aboard the Britannia, Kingston Harbour, July 1976.

State opening of parliament, Ottawa, October 18, 1977, during the queen's Silver Jubilee celebrations in Canada.

so-called "patriation" ceremony from being a fiasco. "Today I have proclaimed the new constitution," Her Majesty said in a nationally televised speech. "There could be no better time for me as, Queen of Canada, to declare again my unbounded confidence in the future of this wonderful country." Replying to a letter of congratulations from Ronald Reagan, Her Majesty wrote that, "This has indeed been an historic day for me as Queen of Canada and for my Government and people of Canada."

In the last decade of the twentieth century, Elizabeth II presided at three more very different Canada Days. On June 30, 1990, she arrived in Ottawa from a spectacular solo Alberta tour. It was a critical time: the previous week the 1987 Meech Lake Accord, an attempt to

The sovereign with her new Canadian cabinet, Rideau Hall, 1984.

On Parliament Hill, Queen Elizabeth II signs the proclamation of the Constitution Act 1982, bringing the revised constitution of Canada into effect, Ottawa, April 17.

Ashley Lubin, Monarchy Canada Photo

Decoration in Ottawa for the proclamation of the revised Constitution of Canada by the queen.

In 1987 the queen praised the settlement reached by federal and provincial governments to reintegrate Quebec into Confederation. This harmonious atmosphere led to Her Majesty's first special tour in Quebec since 1964. Robert Bourassa, Premier of Quebec, welcomed the sovereign "on behalf of the great majority of Quebecers." Replying to his toast, the queen said the accord recognized "that Quebec constitutes a distinct society." Her Majesty and the premier are shown at the Quebec provincial dinner for the queen, 22 October, on the cover of this Canadian periodical.

accommodate Quebec in the 1982 settlement, collapsed. On Parliament Hill, July 1, with the simple words, "I am not just a fair-weather friend, and I am *glad* to be here at this sensitive time," the queen dispelled the cloud of gloom and anxiety hanging over Canadians. Not just the crowd of 40,000 in Ottawa, but the whole country gave a collective sigh of relief at their queen's renewed declaration of faith in Canada's future. Never had the moral authority of a monarch to keep the nation knit together in time of crisis been better demonstrated.

The 1992 Canada Day, the country's 125th July 1, coincided with the queen's ruby jubilee. To mark her forty years as monarch, on June 30 she unveiled the one-and-a-half times life-size equestrian statue of herself on Burmese by Jack Harman, erected on the hill between the centre and east parliament blocks. Once again the sovereign presided at the swearing-in of special appointees to the Queen's Privy Council for Canada. One of the largest crowds in recent Canadian history awaited her arrival on Parliament Hill, again without the Duke of Edinburgh, July 1.

The queen does a walkabout during her 1987 Quebec tour.

Canadian Heritage, Victor Pilon

Signing the royal warrant augmenting her provincial arms in right of British Columbia, Vancouver, 1987.

The queen listens to her seventh Canadian prime minister, Brian Mulroney, during a tour of the Vancouver trade and Convention Centre facilities, October 12, 1987, in prepara-tion for the second Commonwealth Conference of which she has been host as Queen of Canada.

Canadian Heritage, Victor Pilon

Janet Hase, Monarchy Canada Photo

Cutting the cake for the 125th anniversary of confederation, Ottawa, 1992.

Lynne Bell, Monarchy Canada Photo

In 2002, her Golden Jubilee year, the queen attended a nationally televised gala at Roy Thompson Hall, Toronto, where warm tributes by the arts community were paid to Her Majesty, and the audience sang three verses of the royal anthem.

Brian Mulroney, her seventh prime minister, declared, "You have stood, Your Majesty, with Canadians and you have stood by them, and Canadians in turn regard you with loyalty and affection." In stirring words of her own, the queen reminded the nation that, "The real Constitution is not cast immutably on the printed page but lives in the hearts of the people." She called on parliamentarians to "think first and foremost of the national interest" and paid tribute to "our brave Canadian soldiers" serving as peacekeepers in Bosnia. "As Queen of Canada I salute their contribution with appreciation and pride."

On July 1, 1997, the queen arrived in Ottawa from North Bay. She and the Duke of Edinburgh drove onto the hill in the state landau with the sovereign's escort of the Royal Canadian Mounted Police at noon. In her Canada Day speech she reflected on the diversity of Canada and her own widespread travels throughout the land. She urged all Canadians "to make a commitment to help this wonderful nation go from strength to strength as year succeeds year."

Golden Jubilee logo.

On the 2002 Golden Jubilee tour Her Majesty was not asked to open a session of parliament, as she had for the Silver Jubilee, or perform any other constitutional act such as giving royal assent. Enemies of the crown alleged that by the letters patent of 1947, constituting the office of governor general, the sovereign had handed over all royal powers to her representative and could no longer exercise them in Canada. Of course, that was untrue. The letters patent said nothing of the kind. Two governments formed after the new letters patent were promulgated, from the same party — the Liberal Party of Canada — which was responsible for them, had the queen open parliament in 1957 and 1977 (the 1957 opening was arranged by Louis St. Laurent, the queen's first Canadian prime minister, though carried out under her second).

An attack on the crown by the maverick deputy prime minister, John Manley, failed in its object

Celebrating a family anniversary amongst their extended national family, Queen Elizabeth II and the Duke of Edinburgh cut a fiftieth wedding anniversary cake presented to them in Ottawa in 1997.

Janet Huse, Monarchy Canada Photo

and caused such celebrities as Wayne Gretzky and "Stompin'" Tom Connors, hitherto unknown royalists, to voice their support during the Golden Jubilee tour. Her Majesty left her own position in no doubt. "I treasure my place in the life of Canada and my bonds with Canadians everywhere," she said in Vancouver in 2002.

In 2010, the prime minister, Stephen Harper, the queen's eleventh Canadian first minister, had to publicly reprimand the governor general, Michaelle Jean, for describing herself in a speech as Canada's "head of state," even though Elizabeth II's role as Queen of Canada, abroad as well as at home, was clarified and reaffirmed when she presided at the ceremonial rededication of the Vimy Memorial in France, April 9, 2007.

Remarks made by the queen and the prime minister, Stephen Harper, during the 2010 royal tour highlighted Canada as the queen's home. Other events also reinforced that. After greeting the queen and duke on their arrival the governor general, Michaelle Jean, undertook a visit to China, leaving Rideau Hall completely to the queen. After the tour there were media reports that Daniel Lafond, husband of the governor general, had not wanted the royal couple to stay at Rideau Hall, which he vehemently denied. But the alleged insult resulted in the media noting, correctly, that Rideau Hall is, in fact, the queen's house, not the governor general's. The latter is only a tenant while the former is the owner. Unlike viceroys, who only reside in the home for a few years, Rideau Hall has been the queen's home since 1951 for every stay in Ottawa. In 1951 she and the Duke of Edinburgh square danced in its ballroom. On subsequent tours she held investitures and dinners, gave garden parties and planted trees (both of which she did in 2010), and gave audiences to her first ministers, also repeated in 2010 for Stephen Harper. On June 30, two designs were unveiled by the queen at a ceremony in Rideau Hall, one of a window for the senate that will commemorate the diamond jubilees of Elizabeth II and Queen Victoria, and a carved head of her present majesty for the Senate foyer.

Until it was retired in 1997, the other constant of Queen Elizabeth II's Canadian home was the royal yacht *Britannia*. The yacht, commissioned in 1954,

Hilton Hassel's painting of Princess Elizabeth and the Duke of Edinburgh square dancing at Rideau Hall is perhaps the most famous image of the 1951 royal tour.

was not built at the time of the 1951 tour and was not used in 1957, when the queen's stay was limited to Ottawa. Its first trip to Canada was in 1959 and it was used by the queen on tours in 1964, 1967, 1971, 1976, 1983, and 1984.

Also in 2010, a Mi'kmaq cultural event was staged on Halifax Common to celebrate the four hundredth anniversary of Grand Chief Henri Membertou, of the Mi'kmaq First Nation in Nova Scotia, being baptized into the Catholic faith. The event is remembered as an important step in the coming together of the aboriginal and European communities in early Canada. The event focused on the future as well as the history of the Mi'kmaq in Canada.

The queen and the duke's first Canadian event after the arrival ceremony on June 28, 2010, was a tour of the grounds of Halifax Common for the festival. The royal couple engaged in animated conversations with the members of the community as they examined the displays. Starting the tour in this way was appropriate. The queen, like her royal predecessors, has pointedly and appropriately involved and recognized the First

Joining in the Mi'kmaq celebrations in Halifax on June 28, 2010, the queen renewed her close special relationship with the first nations of Canada.

The queen's close relationship with the first nations of Canada brought her to the Six Nations Reserve near Brantford in 1984 to visit Her Majesty's Chapel of the Mohawks. In 2004 she elevated the chapel and Her Majesty's Chapel of the Mohawks in Tyendinaga, near Belleville, to the even higher status of chapels royal, the only two houses of worship in Canada to have been so honoured.

At Calgary in 1990 the queen visited an aboriginal display at the Spruce Meadows Equestrian Centre.

Nations of Canada in the tours and activities of her reign, far beyond what they have often been able to achieve in other areas of public life.

The second day of the 2010 tour featured celebrations marking the one hundredth anniversary of the Royal Canadian Navy, now known as Maritime Command. In Halifax harbour and Bedford Basin the queen — accompanied by the Duke of Edinburgh in the Canadian uniform of a full admiral, the highest ranking naval officer in the Canadian Forces — inspected the international fleet from the bridge of HMCS *St. John's*. The officers and sailors of eight countries manned the sides of their ships and gave three cheers for Her Majesty as she passed each of the more than twenty ships honouring her Canadian naval forces.

This close association with her forces had been repeated in a similar fashion on many occasions in the past half century. As Queen of Canada the command–in-chief of the armed forces is vested in Her Majesty by virtue of the declaration in the Constitution Act. In addition, the queen is colonel-in-chief of some sixteen corps/branches and regiments in the land force. On her numerous tours of Canada, the men and women of the forces provided countless guards of honours and royal salutes in all parts of the country and for all sorts of ceremonial events.

Corporal Johanie Maheu, Formation Imaging Services, Halifax, Nova Scotia/Department of National Defence

During the international fleet review at Halifax on June 29, 2010, celebrating the one hundredth anniversary of the Royal Canadian Navy, the queen inspected a naval guard of honour on HMCS St. John's.

The queen drives in state to her first Dominion Day (Canada Day) on Parliament Hill, 1 July 1959, escorted by the RCMP.

Presenting new colours to the Argyll and Sutherland Highlanders of Canada (Princess Louise's), July 1, on the hill.

In 1959 the queen presented the Queen's Colour to the Royal Canadian Navy as part of ceremonies that included an even larger international fleet review in Halifax harbour than in 2010.

The queen inspected a guard of honour from the 48th Highlanders of Canada in Toronto in 1997. The regiment is one the sixteen units of which the queen is colonel-in-chief.

Lisa Mitchell, Monarchy Canada Photo

A few events, like the 2010 fleet review, stand out. In 1959, Queen Elizabeth II dedicated the memorial in Ottawa to the airmen of the Commonwealth. That same year the Canadian Guards presented a changing of the guard ceremony in Ottawa as they mounted guard for the first time at the queen's residence in Canada, Rideau Hall, a practice carried out every summer since by the regiment and subsequently by the reserve guards regiments of Canada. Also in 1959 the queen conducted a naval fleet review similar to the one in 2010. In 1984 she visited the Canadian war cemetery in Normandy and received the French president, François Mitterrand, as Queen of Canada. In 2007 she rededicated the Vimy Ridge memorial, again as Queen of Canada.

Each portion of the 2010 tour included an event of national significance. In Winnipeg, where the queen and her husband arrived from Ottawa on Saturday, July 3, after enjoying a day's holiday at Meech Lake, the event

The pomp and pageantry of royal sporting events was evident at the 1973 Queen's Plate in Toronto.

Michael Burns

Janet Huse, Monarchy Canada Photo

2010 Queen's Plate winning jockey, Eurico Rosa da Silva, originally from Brazil, received his trophy from the queen with Latin graciousness as equally thrilled owner Don Romeo (left) and trainer Nicholas Gonzalez (right) enjoyed their moment with the queen in the winner's circle at Woodbine following the victory by Big Red Mike.

The Queen of Canada drops in on Chicago, July 6, 1959. Red ensigns and Union Jacks decorated the windy city's streets for Her Majesty's visit to the Trade Fair.

Above: *One of the many ceremonies carried out by the queen at Rideau Hall, her home in Ottawa, was the investiture of her incoming governor general, Jules Léger, with the Order of Canada in 1973.*

Right: *In 1976 the queen opened the Summer Olympics in Montreal, the biggest sporting event held in Canada up to that time.*

was the unveiling of the cornerstone of the Canadian Museum for Human Rights. The queen has a well-known record as a supporter of human rights, especially in Africa. It is the first new national museum built in Canada in over forty years and the first located outside the Ottawa-Gatineau region. This national centre of learning will be located at The Forks, the junction of the Red and Assiniboine rivers in downtown Winnipeg. The cornerstone that was laid comes from Runnymede, where King John sealed the Magna Carta in 1215.

Sports also played a part in the 2010 tour. Her Majesty and the Duke of Edinburgh attended the 151st running of the Queen's Plate on July 4 in Toronto. It was the 150th anniversary of Queen Victoria's establishment of the Plate, which is North America's oldest continuously run horse race, and the fourth time that Queen Elizabeth II had attended. The other years were 1959, 1973, and 1997. Her parents had also attended the race in 1939. The 2010 edition was filled with the same pageantry that has marked the race for decades with the royal arrival in a horse-drawn landau, an escort by the Royal Canadian Mounted Police and the Toronto Police Mounted Unit, and the regimental band of the Governor General's Horse Guards, of which the queen is colonel-in-chief, providing the music.

The queen has attended hockey, football, and lacrosse games in Canada. She watched the Calgary Stampede twice, opened the 1976 Olympics Games in Montreal, and closed the Commonwealth Games

An iconic moment in Canada was when the Queen of Canada dropped the puck at the ceremonial opening of a Vancouver Canucks hockey game on October 7, 2002.

twice, in Edmonton in 1978 and in Victoria in 1994. On October 7, 2002, in an iconic Canadian moment, the queen dropped the ceremonial puck at a Vancouver Canucks hockey game.

At the July 5, 2010, state dinner in Toronto the prime minister, Stephen Harper, reminded the guests of that moment in Vancouver. He also noted the recent gold-medal victory by what he rightly described as the queen's Canadian national hockey team. As one of the gifts to the queen to mark the tour he asked Her Majesty to unveil a new exhibit for the Hockey Hall of Fame. To the surprised delight of the audience the exhibit included a Canadian team jersey with the queen's royal cypher on the back where a player's name usually appears. This represented the queen's status as, in the prime minister's words, "Canada's MVP [most valuable player]."

The royal family historically, and Queen Elizabeth II personally, have been at the forefront of new communications and transportation technologies. Whether it was Queen Victoria's early use of railways to travel throughout the United Kingdom, her children's similar use of the steel roads to traverse the continent that was her Canadian domain, King Edward VII being one of the first people to own an automobile, or King George V making the new communications innovation of the wireless (radio) his own, they saw technology as a means of more easily reaching their worldwide subjects.

In 1951 Princess Elizabeth became the first member of the royal family to fly across the Atlantic in a commercial airliner when she arrived in Canada on a BOAC Stratocruiser. She was making virtue out of a necessity as the tour had been delayed a couple of weeks and she was making up the time that would have been spent on a sea voyage as planned. In 1957 the queen made her first television broadcast as she addressed her Canadian people from Ottawa at Thanksgiving. It proved a trial run for the subsequent switch from radio to television for her broadcast to the Commonwealth the following Christmas. At Expo '67 she travelled on the innovative minirail.

The BlackBerry smartphone, developed by the Waterloo, Ontario, company Research In Motion,

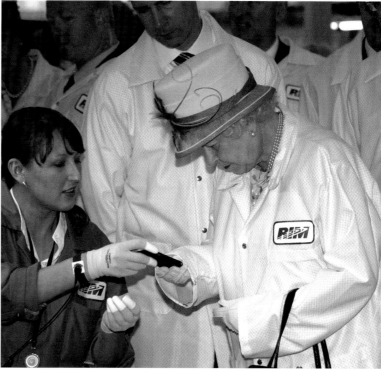

The queen visited Research In Motion, producers of the world famous BlackBerry, at their Waterloo, Ontario, headquarters on July 5, 2010.

Tim Rooke/Rex Features

headed by Jim Balsillie, himself an honorary captain in the queen's Canadian naval forces, has taken the world by storm in the twenty-first century. To highlight this Canadian achievement a visit to the RIM headquarters in Waterloo was arranged for the 2010 tour and Her Majesty was presented with her own BlackBerry. It was later reported in the media that, not surprisingly, she already owned one.

In the afternoon the queen visited the new Pinewood film studios in Toronto, the largest in Canada. There, among other activities, she donned special glasses to view a 3D film in production and saw archival 3D footage of her own coronation in 1953, which had only been rediscovered recently.

Top left: *The queen's first television broadcast was her Thanksgiving message to Canadians from Ottawa in 1957.*

Bottom right: *Queen Elizabeth II, the Duke of Edinburgh, and Dalton McGuinty, premier of Ontario, donned special 3D glasses at Pinewood Film Studios in Toronto.*

Janet Huse, Monarchy Canada Photo

However, as beneficial as technology has been to royal tours nothing is as special as the royal walkabout, which the queen's mother, Queen Elizabeth, consort of King George VI, had initiated in Ottawa on the great 1939 royal tour, and which Queen Elizabeth II has made her own throughout her long reign. The term "interactive" is used in the modern world to describe computer programs, but a walkabout is truly interactive.

A monarchical society is not one where one person rules on his or her own, it is one in which there is a bond between sovereign and subjects who each play their essential role in making society work. That bond was on display in the summer of 2010.

The crowds out to see the queen and the duke were as large, and in some cases larger, than those that had turned out for the queen when she was a much younger monarch.

The newest member of a Canadian family was introduced to the queen in 1976.

Huge crowds in Ottawa watched the queen unveil a statue of the great Canadian jazz pianist Oscar Peterson on June 30, 2010.

Janet Huse, Monarchy Canada Photo

A constant support to the queen in her tours of Canada, Prince Philip, Duke of Edinburgh has also maintained his own significant involvement in Canadian life. On July 5, 2010, he presented Duke of Edinburgh Awards to young Canadians. He created the Award Scheme in 1959 to promote social activities by young people throughout the Commonwealth.

The day the queen arrived in Halifax it was cold and raining. It had been raining heavily for hours but the crowds were still there waiting. Two days later, in staid Ottawa, it was sunnier but a workday. Yet so many thousands of people turned out to see Her Majesty unveil a statue of pianist Oscar Peterson outside the National Arts Centre, that one side of Elgin Street had to be closed down to accommodate the numbers. A twelve-year-old girl who had the opportunity to present flowers to the sovereign told a reporter that it was the highlight of her life that she would someday tell her children and grandchildren about. At the Canada Day celebrations on Parliament Hill the next day, media commentators stated that the crowds were triple the normal numbers for the annual July 1 celebrations.

By the time the royal couple reached Toronto the warmth of summer had turned into the city's first heat wave in three years. The temperatures were in the mid-30s (Celsius) with a humidex of over 40°C. An overheated transformer exploded and caused a major power blackout in downtown Toronto, including the Royal York Hotel where the Duke of Edinburgh was presiding at a ceremony for his Award Scheme on July 5.

The heat had not let up on July 6 when the queen and duke arrived at Queen's Park for a good citizenship awards ceremony and official farewell before they would leave for New York, where the queen would address the United Nations, just as she had in 1957. Leaving from Toronto reminded the world of her role as Canadian sovereign as well as sovereign of fifteen other U.N. countries.

The week before there had been heat of a different sort in Toronto. The downtown core had seen

In 1983, Victoria, British Columbia, was the location for just one of the innumerable huge crowds that have greeted the queen throughout Canada and throughout her reign.

British Columbia Government: B. Novak

The queen undertook one of her classic walkabouts in Halifax in 1994.

unprecedented security as a vast area was cordoned off by a high fence for the G20 heads of government conference. Large crowds of demonstrators turned out at several locations, including Queen's Park. In the crowd of thousands, a criminal element bent on destruction for destruction's sake had intermingled with legitimate demonstrators. The police response was both praised as appropriate and criticized as either heavy-handed or inadequate. Over eight hundred people were arrested. Though events of that type are not unusual elsewhere in the world experience, they were unprecedented in Toronto. Ontario's premier, Dalton McGuinty, claimed that the city had been "scarred" by the violence and destruction.

The passage of a week could have been the passage of an eternity. Once again thousands of people had turned out, braving the oppressive heat and humidity, but there was neither hatred nor fear in the air. This time there was celebration instead of protest. There were security barriers lining the route of the queen's walkabout, but they were hardly a barrier between queen and people. On the CBC it was noted that unlike at the G20, people stormed the barricades merely to present flowers to the queen.

In the Halifax, Ottawa, Winnipeg, or Toronto celebrations in 1959, or any other year, there were the same seniors, the same middle aged Canadians, the same young people and the same children with their flowers or other gifts. The queen's events in Canada are like other family occasions, transcending the varied activities and interests that usually separate the generations. They bring people of the national family together regardless of age, through their affection and loyalty for their common sovereign.

What was significant about the crowds at the walkabouts in 2010 however was the fact that they were not new. The queen had changed, from the 1951 princess to the 1957 young queen to the self-assured 1970s sovereign to the middle-aged monarch of the 1980s and finally to the matronly grandmother royal figure of the twenty-first century. The fashions of the people had changed with the decades, their ethnicity was more diverse, the older people of the early reign

174

The queen had just arrived at Yellowknife airport in 1994 and was already overloaded with flowers of welcome.

were gone, and the young had grown older with the queen. Otherwise, the crowds looked the same.

The royal tours from 1786 to the present have taken that simple but profound concept and extended it, not just to the several generations living at one time but to the even greater number of generations living over several centuries. And those generations are not united by just a continuing institution, which the crown of course is, but by the same continuing family. In undertaking her 2010 royal tour of Canada, and planning for her next, Queen Elizabeth II was not just following in the footsteps of people who held her office of monarch, she was following in the footsteps of her great-great-great-grandfather and her great-great-great-granduncle and all her family since. This merger of national history and family history in Canada has given substance to the declarations made by the royal family when they have come to Canada over the past two-and-a-quarter centuries that they truly have come home.

At the farewell walkabout at Queen's Park, Toronto on July 6, 2010, another huge crowd engulfed the queen.

Janet Huse, Monarchy Canada Photo

A glorious glimpse of Canadian royal pageantry. Arrival of the queen at Parliament Hill for the 1990 Canada Day festivities.

Garry Toffoli, Monarchy Canada Photo

Eight Generations of Royal Tours

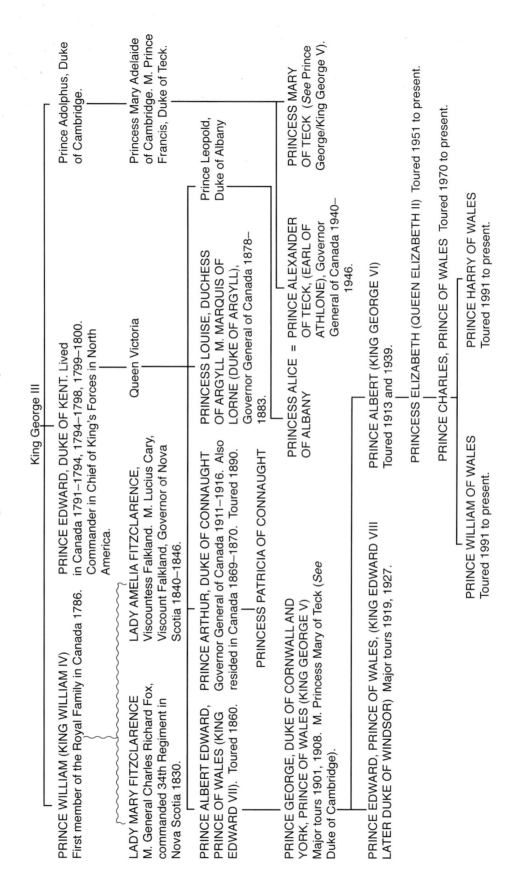

King George III

PRINCE EDWARD, DUKE OF KENT. Lived in Canada 1791–1794, 1794–1798, 1799–1800. Commander in Chief of King's Forces in North America.

Prince Adolphus, Duke of Cambridge.

Princess Mary Adelaide of Cambridge. M. Prince Francis, Duke of Teck.

PRINCE WILLIAM (KING WILLIAM IV). First member of the Royal Family in Canada 1786.

LADY MARY FITZCLARENCE. M. General Charles Richard Fox, commanded 34th Regiment in Nova Scotia 1830.

LADY AMELIA FITZCLARENCE, Viscountess Falkland. M. Lucius Cary, Viscount Falkland, Governor of Nova Scotia 1840–1846.

Queen Victoria

PRINCESS LOUISE, DUCHESS OF ARGYLL. M. MARQUIS OF LORNE (DUKE OF ARGYLL), Governor General of Canada 1878–1883.

Prince Leopold, Duke of Albany

PRINCESS MARY OF TECK (*See* Prince George/King George V).

PRINCE ALBERT EDWARD, PRINCE OF WALES (KING EDWARD VII). Toured 1860.

PRINCE ARTHUR, DUKE OF CONNAUGHT Governor General of Canada 1911–1916. Toured 1890. Also resided in Canada 1869–1870.

PRINCESS ALICE OF ALBANY

PRINCE ALEXANDER OF TECK, (EARL OF ATHLONE), Governor General of Canada 1940– 1946.

=

PRINCESS PATRICIA OF CONNAUGHT

PRINCE GEORGE, DUKE OF CORNWALL AND YORK, PRINCE OF WALES (KING GEORGE V) Major tours 1901, 1908. M. Princess Mary of Teck (*See* Duke of Cambridge).

PRINCE ALBERT (KING GEORGE VI) Toured 1913 and 1939.

PRINCE EDWARD, PRINCE OF WALES, (KING EDWARD VIII LATER DUKE OF WINDSOR) Major tours 1919, 1927.

PRINCESS ELIZABETH (QUEEN ELIZABETH II) Toured 1951 to present.

PRINCE CHARLES, PRINCE OF WALES Toured 1970 to present.

PRINCE WILLIAM OF WALES Toured 1991 to present.

PRINCE HARRY OF WALES Toured 1991 to present.

INDEX